Daughters of Rizpah

Daughters of Rizpah

Nonviolence and the Transformation of Trauma

SHARON A. BUTTRY
and DANIEL L. BUTTRY

Foreword by
MOLLY T. MARSHALL

CASCADE *Books* • Eugene, Oregon

DAUGHTERS OF RIZPAH
Nonviolence and the Transformation of Trauma

Cascade Books
An Imprint of Wipf and Stock Publishers
199 W. 8th Ave., Suite 3
Eugene, OR 97401

www.wipfandstock.com

PAPERBACK ISBN: 978-1-5326-9931-3
HARDCOVER ISBN: 978-1-5326-9932-0
EBOOK ISBN: 978-1-5326-9933-7

Cataloguing-in-Publication data:

Names: Buttry, Sharon A., author. | Buttry, Daniel L., author. | Marshall, Molly T., foreword.

Title: Daughters of Rizpah : nonviolence and the transformation of trauma / Sharon A. Buttry and Daniel L. Buttry ; foreword by Molly T. Marshall.

Description: Eugene, OR : Cascade Books, 2020 | Includes bibliographical references.

Identifiers: ISBN 978-1-5326-9931-3 (paperback) | ISBN 978-1-5326-9932-0 (hardcover) | ISBN 978-1-5326-9933-7 (ebook)

Subjects: LCSH: Psychic trauma—Biblical teaching. | Suffering in the Bible. | Stress (Psychology). | Psychic trauma. | Nonviolence. | Social change.

Classification: BF575.S75 B88 2020 (print) | BF575.S75 B88 (ebook)

Manufactured in the U.S.A.   OCTOBER 8, 2020

This book is dedicated
to all the courageous
Daughters of Rizpah
whoever and wherever
they may be.

CONTENTS

ILLUSTRATIONS

FOREWORD

In the world of global peacemaking, Sharon A. and Daniel L. Buttry are revered leaders. They have given their lives to issues of justice, always working to promote gospel values while finding ways to work across ecclesial and faith tradition boundaries. They recognize the work of God in the many pathways for seeking peace, as this book demonstrates. They have served as American Baptists's letters of recommendation in the global community as they build relationships that bring healing and offer new initiatives from leaders they have mentored.

Central Baptist Theological Seminary has drawn on the wisdom of these two transformative leaders. We saw the fruit of their labors, especially in their work to form a new generation of women and men who will extend their work in conflict transformation. Indeed, to honor their life work, we instituted the Buttry Center for Peace and Nonviolence at our seminary.

Taking a rather obscure story from the Hebrew Bible, the story of Rizpah's protest against the raw violence and indignity wreaked upon her sons, the Buttrys have used this text to illuminate how it is possible to recover from trauma. Through the lens of 2 Sam 21, a grisly narrative of interethnic violence, revenge, and recompense, they examine the varied roles of victim/survivor, aggressor/offender, with an eye to construct a hopeful future story.

Aware of the significant new studies in Post Traumatic Growth (that moves beyond the normative analysis of PTSD), the authors outline what concrete steps are possible to move from the cycle of violence, that empower victims to take agency and nonviolent actions that ultimately have the power to challenge and change the oppressor. This work aligns well with the service of those involved in "trauma informed practice" through psychotherapy, counseling, and social work.

They do not shy away from hard theological questions such as: "Where is God in trauma?" They wisely know that the problem of evil cannot be resolved with platitudes or simplistic answers; they have seen too much in the world, from Burma/Myanmar to Lebanon, from Nagaland to Liberia, from Bosnia to Sri Lanka, and points beyond. They do recognize where God is at work, clearly.

This accessible text is far from simply theoretical. After a close and perceptive reading of the story of Rizpah, they offer stories of the daughters of Rizpah drawn from the discrete communities where they have borne witness to peacemaking. The steps from victimhood that seeks revenge to claiming agency that empowers a new story of hope are outlined in the stories of remarkable women who have turned their suffering and tragic loss into a horizon of hope.

The authors include varied resources that help the reader move from these pages to action in their communities. A training toolbox, a sample sermon, poetry and art about Rizpah, and the work of biblical commentators on this text comprise the kind of material agents of peacemaking require. It is an aggregation of significant and pertinent information.

I am grateful for this curated wisdom that arises from the expansive practice of pursuing peace. Using the biblical story of Rizpah offers a way of reading Scripture that allows both new insight and a pattern for transforming violence into a life-giving future. The Buttrys have offered a wonderful portrait of what is possible.

—Dr. Molly T. Marshall
Retired President and Professor of Theology and Spiritual Formation
Central Baptist Theological Seminary
Shawnee, Kansas

ACKNOWLEDGMENTS

No book is a solo project, or, as in this case, a duo project. This book in particular is a community project. There are so many people we wish to acknowledge and thank for their contribution to our journey.

We deeply appreciate the people at Wipf and Stock Publishers for taking on this book and working carefully with us to publish it. Thanks especially to our editor Charlie Collier for his patience and guidance as we worked together through all the details of the editing process, especially for his precise answers to our questions.

We honor Rev. Cindy Weber, a pastor from Louisville who preached about Rizpah at a Baptist Peace Fellowship of North America conference we attended many years ago. She focused on the nonviolent resistance of Rizpah, but for us she awakened an interest that grew ever deeper the more we got into the story. Rev. Weber has pastored Jeff Street Baptist Community at Liberty in Louisville, Kentucky, for more than three decades. Jeff Street is committed to justice, mercy, inclusivity, creativity, and community.

We are especially grateful to Suthasini Suthakaran from Sri Lanka, Rosette Mansour from Lebanon, as well as Neidonuo Angami, Khesheli Chishi, and the other amazing Naga women we met in our travels throughout northeast India. These women shared their stories with us with great humility, but in ways that have profoundly inspired us. They are living examples to us of the way that trauma can be transformed with power and grace.

Thanks to Jude Sutharshan who introduced Dan to Sutha and then translated for Dan's interviews with her. Besides having been Principal of the seminary that Sutha attended, Jude works passionately for healing and reconciliation in the wake of the Sri Lankan Civil War.

We deeply appreciate the work of Eastern Mennonite University and their Seminars on Trauma Awareness and Recovery (STAR) program. STAR opened up for us so many of the technical aspects of trauma, its impact, and the way toward transformation. We give thanks to the good folks at Conflict Transformation Program at EMU and to Olga Botcharova for permission to use the three diagrams related to the trauma cycles and the trauma healing journey.

Thanks to Molly Marshall for reading the text and writing the Foreword. Dr. Marshall has offered support and encouragement for us in our work over the years as well as serving as an advocate, role model, and guide for many women in finding their prophetic voices.

Thanks to our dear friend Jan Krist for use of her song "Hope." Even more we appreciate Jan for being one of the prophets of hope in her music. Her songs are the sound track for much of our peacemaking work.

Thanks to friend and scholar Matthijs Kronemeijer, originally from The Netherlands, for introducing us to the hymn by fellow Dutch theologian Huub Oosterhuis as well as translating the hymn into English. Thanks to Father Oosterhuis for permission to include his hymn in this book, including approving Matthijs's translation.

Thanks to Diana Francis, a British Quaker and peacemaker who worked with Dan on Naga peacemaking efforts in northeast India. Diana has been forwarding daily news briefs put together by a British Quaker working group, which has helped us stay informed of the activities of the Naga Mothers.

Thanks to our son Jonathan Mayo-Buttry of Wise Visuals for his assistance in getting the diagrams and art works prepared for the printing process.

Thanks to our friend and colleague Ruth Mooney for helping us understand the use of some of the Spanish names in our text.

Thanks to our friend Ken Sehested who also served as pastor of our Mission Partnership Team. Ken has been our poetic prophet, though in this case he read the manuscript and caught some editing details. He also introduced us to the data about generational trauma.

We appreciate the encouragement we have received from David Crumm of Read the Spirit and Front Edge Publications. David edited and published four of Dan's earlier books and a book with a chapter by Sharon. David has consistently encouraged us in our writing. He is a selfless, kind friend.

Thanks to all our workshop participants over the years who helped us refine our understanding of this story as their dramatized interviews and questions helped us discover new dimensions to the ancient story of Rizpah. We also deeply appreciate all the individuals and congregations who donated for our support in our peacemaking mission work. We couldn't have learned as much, touched as many people, or discovered folks like Sutha, Rosette, or the Naga women without such a sending community.

We are profoundly grateful to International Ministries (IM) of the American Baptists Churches. We developed the core concepts in this book and met some of the Daughters of Rizpah while serving as Global Servants with IM. The financial and professional support we received through being part of IM made our journey of peacemaking possible, including the aspects of our work that took shape in this book. We appreciate the Executive Directors under whom we worked, the Area Directors who guided us, and the financial folks who moved the money to make our work happen. We deeply love and appreciate our Global Servants colleagues who joined us in our trainings and often worked alongside us, sometimes providing us with new insights into this ancient story.

Most of all we are grateful in the core of our being to the God of hope who raised Christ from the dead, thus assuring that no trauma, however horrific it may be, will have the last word. That is the hope that has undergirded and driven all that we do.

ABBREVIATIONS

Gen   Genesis
Exod   Exodus
Deut   Deuteronomy
Josh   Joshua
1 Sam 1 Samuel
2 Sam 2 Samuel
1 Kgs 1 Kings
2 Kgs 2 Kings
1 Chr 1 Chronicles
Ps   Psalms
Isa   Isaiah
Jer   Jeremiah
Ezek   Ezekiel
Matt   Matthew
Rom   Romans

INTRODUCTION

DAN WAS LEADING A workshop in Myanmar, commonly known as Burma, during some of the worst days of the military dictatorship. These workshops were called "conflict transformation trainings," but they also included a section on nonviolent struggle. Dan used a series of Bible stories about nonviolent actions. One of those stories was that of Rizpah found in 2 Sam 21:1–14.

The workshop participants were divided into groups of five or six with each group assigned one of the Bible stories. Each group had thirty minutes to grapple with the biblical text guided by a worksheet with questions. Then the groups reported out to the whole. The last group to report was the group that studied 2 Sam 21.

That group's spokesperson was a young woman from one of the ethnic minority groups out of which an insurgency had engaged in a protracted violent struggle against the dominant Burmese-controlled government. In her entire lifetime her people had known only war and repression.

She rose from her chair in the circle of the group and began going through the worksheet questions, telling about the characters and the story in the Bible study. Then she got to the final question, which she read aloud: "Who is today's Rizpah?" She paused. She straightened herself and stood a little taller. She threw back her shoulders and in a clear, commanding voice announced, "Aung San Suu Kyi is today's Rizpah!"

The moment was electric. Most people in the US have no idea who Aung San Suu Kyi is. She is the daughter of Aung San, the father of Burmese independence. Aung San was assassinated in 1947 on the eve of independence when his daughter was two years old. She spent much of her early life in India and England, but returned to Burma in 1988 to care for her ailing mother just as political upheaval exploded into a major national crisis. Aung San Suu Kyi entered into the massive demonstrations for democracy and quickly became one of the leading spokespersons.

The military launched a brutal countercoup in September 1988, and the forces of democracy were temporarily pushed back. The military called for an election in 1990, and Suu Kyi ran to be prime minister. Her party, the National League for Democracy, won the vote by a landslide, but the military invalidated the election. Earlier in 1989 Suu Kyi was placed under house arrest, and she was confined for almost fifteen of the next twenty-one years. She became one of the most prominent political prisoners in the world, and was named for the Nobel Peace Prize in 1991. After years of struggle her party was legalized and won power in the Parliament in 2012. Though not allowed to be Prime Minister, Suu Kyi won a seat in the Parliament and has become the guiding voice for the government of Myanmar (now with serious implications of condoning and defending mass violence and even genocide against the Rohingya people in the border area with Bangladesh).

But all that was still in the distant and impossible-to-imagine future. When Dan was in Myanmar in the early 2000s Aung San Suu Kyi was still under house arrest, embodying the faint dream of democracy. The powerful grip of the military over life in Myanmar was as strong as ever. There was no free press, and the military-controlled papers never mentioned her name. People would not dare to speak her name in any public conversation. The only time Dan heard her name spoken inside Myanmar, actually seldom even her name but rather "her" or "the lady," was in side conversation whispers.

Yet in that workshop this young woman was prompted by the story of Rizpah to stand proudly and proclaim boldly, "Aung San

Suu Kyi is today's Rizpah!" This biblical story is largely unknown to most Christian and Jewish people in the Western world. The story draws on historic treaties between Israel and geographic ethnic groups outside the covenant between God and Israel. Kings Saul and David are the main characters. David tries to appease God and the ethnic Gibeonites to bring an end to a famine in Israel. He slays seven of the remaining "sons" of Saul. Five sons belonged to a daughter of Saul, Merab. Two sons belonged to Rizpah, one of Saul's concubines. Merab remains silent when her sons are executed. God is silent, too, as the famine continues.

Rizpah mourns her two sons publicly, keeping the birds of the air and the wild animals away from the decaying bodies of her sons. Her vigil continues for several months and eventually attracts David's attention. His response to Rizpah completes David's own mourning as he takes responsibility for the bones of Saul, his dear friend Jonathan, as well as the sons of Rizpah and Merab. After David gives proper honor to the remains of the deceased members of Saul's family, ending the cycles of violence, then God responds. The rains come, restoring the land, and ending the famine.

What was it in that ancient story that gave strength to this young woman from Myanmar to courageously speak truth into a context ruled by fear? How could such an obscure, strange story mobilize a woman to a highly risky, incisive pronouncement? The story is indeed obscure. Rizpah's actions are described in a mere four verses of 2 Sam 21, easily missed in a quick read through of the Bible, and rarely, if ever, addressed in a lifetime of listening to Sunday sermons.

As a mother, Rizpah has lost what is most precious to her, and she has no hope of her sons being restored to her. However, Rizpah does not step aside. Instead, she steps into the power of her grief and takes action without strategy or partners. She acts from her passionate heart as a mother, and the result turns out to be history-shaking and history-making. Rizpah speaks to us today that we can explore our feelings and our passions and resist the temptation to say, "I am alone and can't do anything to confront injustice."

Constructive change and justice rarely come from the top down. Rizpah's actions surprise us. She is a most unlikely change agent in the schemes of government or politics. She had been the concubine, basically a sex slave, of the former King Saul. In terms of the world, she is powerless. However, observing Rizpah, the secret of power from the margins is affirmed. Her power is in her bold and public cries of grief. Her power matches the depths of pain she has experienced. Where does hope come from in hopeless situations? The power of hope sings out through Rizpah's commands to the birds and dogs to leave her children alone. She may not be able to control the action of a king, but she can shout out from the power of her impassioned grief to the destructive natural forces that threaten the bodies of her sons.

Part of the power of the story is that Rizpah's actions are described as taking place from the "beginning of the harvest until rain fell on them from the heavens," a period of months rather than days. Her perseverance, audacity, and courage are easily overlooked at first glance. However, when we take the time to dramatize the story and explore all the dynamics an amazing picture emerges. Rizpah employed nonviolent, transformative action in a seemingly hopeless situation. After all, her sons were dead, and she could not bring them back. She had no guarantee that King David would notice her public protest, though her neighbors surely must have noticed and thought she had completely lost her mind. One can imagine that after a while they just looked the other way.

In this book we want to resist looking away and instead take you deep into the story. We will unpack the power of Rizpah's action that led to the transformation of King David's heart and eventually brought God's favor and the end of famine. We will explore the story through the various angles of trauma, both personal and social, and explore what reconciliation looks like based on the rewriting of trauma's story. Finally, we will bring the story into the present with stories of modern "Daughters of Rizpah." We hope your heart will be open to the "Rizpah" in you and that you will encourage others to be the next "Daughters of Rizpah."

Part I

TERRIBLE STORIES

KAREN BLIXEN UNDER HER pen name Isak Dinesen said, "All sorrows can be borne if you put them into a story."[1] Human suffering can be a matter of pure misery, but a story begins to explore the meaning of difficult or awful events for our lives. We may not be able to articulate that meaning, but how we tell the story expresses some of the feelings involved. How we set forth the narration gives the arc of events and structure to something that may have been overwhelming and seemingly formless.

In this section, we briefly look at the way we tell and use terrible stories. Then we begin the plunge into one particular terrible story found within the sacred texts of Judaism and Christianity. That such a story could be found in a sacred text indicates that there is some larger meaning to this dreadful narrative. In our own journeys we have learned that redemptive meaning can only be found by a deep dive into the horror, into the heart of darkness. There in the depths, a light shines.

1. Mohn, "Talk with Isak Dinesen."

1

DEALING WITH TERRIBLE STORIES

STORYTELLING IS SUCH AN important part of culture and has immense social value. Through stories, we pass on family and social history. Through stories, we share values, information, and preserve the nuances of humanity in all its diversity. Stories can evoke so many deep emotions in us. We love stories, especially with happy endings. We have a friend who only watches movies and listens to stories with guaranteed happy endings.

Yet we are bombarded daily in social media, news, Facebook posts, and documentaries with terrible stories. These are stories that describe suffering and shame, stories that make us want to turn the page, change the channel, or turn the radio off. They may be stories that make us click "angry" or "sad" icons.

History is full of terrible stories, many of them around experiences of war. Terrible stories such as the Holocaust in World War II are so overwhelming that many people even seek to deny what happened. Sometimes we try to sanitize stories, such as making slavery in the United States sound benign so that US citizens, especially white citizens, don't have to acknowledge the terrible chapter of our national story that still haunts our political and social life today.

We have our own intimate stories, those "skeletons in the closet" and "family secrets" that may or may not be shared or believed among family members. Families will go to great lengths to keep these stories hidden because they are often full of shame and humiliation. They go against our self-image as good people.

Sacred texts are no exception, and it is here that we find the story of Rizpah. It is a story of genocide, revenge, execution, mourning, and madness. It is an ancient story, yet full of concerns that jump out in contemporary news. Is there nothing new under the sun?

What do we do with these stories? We can ignore them and miss the opportunity that such stories provide. We can re-enact terrible stories within our own lives or project them into the lives of others, continuing the suffering and heartache that comes with unresolved trauma. The body remembers trauma, and even if we don't act consciously trauma can leak into the next generation in very unhealthy patterns. Family and national history thus repeats, recycles, and may even intensify, creating new trauma and ongoing terrible stories.

There is another way to deal with terrible stories, the way of transformation. Someone "flips the script." Someone acts out of turn and breaks the established rules. Someone takes a path of courage and creativity, and a new story emerges. Happy endings are one thing, but when good comes out of evil and lives are transformed, bringing hope and reconciliation—now that is a truly good story! Let's take a closer look at a terrible story in a sacred text and see the transformation from terror to trust. It is a story for the ages.

2

A TERRIBLE STORY IN THE BIBLE

THE BIBLE HAS MANY wonderful and inspiring stories, whether parables told by Jesus or stories of various characters in biblical history. But there are also some hideous stories of violence, abuse, and degradation in the Bible. Phyllis Trible called such stories, "texts of terror" in her book of that title that examined in depth four horrible stories of violence against women.[1]

The stories of David have been told to children for centuries: Stories of the shepherd boy protecting his sheep by killing lions and bears, the story of the young boy slaying Goliath with his shepherd's sling, of David becoming the mighty king and writing beautiful psalms. But David's story has a more sordid side that we don't tell children: His "affair" (some even take it as rape) with Bathsheba and then the plot to kill her husband, the violence and civil war with his children, and dancing nearly naked when he brought the ark to Jerusalem. These stories have moral messages for us, but sometimes those messages are complex and even unclear as the stories raise moral ambiguities. The story of Rizpah is even worse.

At first blush, it is easy to read this story as some sort of violent payback to the family of Saul for their own violence. David

1. Trible, *Texts of Terror*.

5

is just settling the score in response to God's demand for justice. But in the end, there is a tender moment to comfort the grieving mother of those killed. Such is the perspective that most of the Bible commentaries on 1 and 2 Samuel take about the story.[2]

But let's not linger too long with this strange story of David and Rizpah, because the more we think about it the more disturbing it becomes. Those killed were not complicit in the genocide of Saul, so is God demanding human sacrifice? Are children to be killed for the sins of their father? The wild fury of Rizpah's grief suggests that all is not well. Can a killer say "there, there" to the mourning survivors, and everything will return to normal?

The more we dig into the story the more questions are raised, troubling questions. So we quickly turn the page and get on to the "good stuff." Where is the inspiring story? Remember, David is a good guy, so let's get to the passages that show him in a good light or at least a redeeming light.

This text, however, rewards those who are willing to sit with it and dig deeper into it, as uncomfortable as that will be. The rapid glance at the story wearing pro-David glasses just brings confusion that causes readers to look away. However, if readers take off those pro-David glasses and peer deeply into the text, if they don't just read it but feel it, and even live it, then they will find a very different story emerging. They can discover a story of good news arriving from an unlikely place. Readers can enter a story of powerful transformation out of horror, a story of reconciliation and hope. Yet this transformative story is one that can't be seen unless the reader is willing to follow the plot into the depths of rage and despair.

To summarize the story in 2 Sam 21:1–14, there is a famine in Israel. David prays, and God speaks to him that Israel is guilty of having shed innocent blood, specifically that Saul had massacred Gibeonites, people of an ethnic minority group within Israel. David met with surviving Gibeonites to ask how to make things right.

---

2. For example, see Youngblood, *1 & 2 Samuel*, 1056; Bergen, *1, 2 Samuel*, 446; Keil and Delitzsch, *Biblical Commentary*, 462–63; Baldwin, *1 & 2 Samuel*, 284–85; Arnold, *1 & 2 Samuel*, 620; Thompson, *Penitence and Sacrifice*, 115.

The Gibeonites refuse financial compensation and instead ask that seven of Saul's male descendants be executed. David concurs, sparing Jonathan's son. The seven young men, perhaps even boys, were killed publicly as a religious ritual, "before the Lord."

Rizpah, mother of two of the slain young men, began a vigil by the bodies, driving away the scavenging birds and dogs. David hears about Rizpah's action. He first goes to the village of Jabesh-giliad to gather the bones of Saul and the sons who had been killed in the earlier battle at Mt. Gilboa. The bodies of Saul and his slain warrior sons had been hung up on a Philistine city wall following the Philistine victory. The men of Jabesh-giliad stealthily took down the bodies and held them for safekeeping in their village. With those bones David comes to the execution ground, gathers the bones of those killed, and likely with Rizpah and others in the family of Saul, buried all the bones in the ancestral lands. The story then concludes with God answering the prayers for the land, presumably ending the famine.

What an awful story! You are invited to risk entering into it with the full feeling of the characters and plunging into its depths to see where the redemptive story might emerge. Here is the text of 2 Sam 21:1–14 as translated in the New Revised Standard Version:

> 21 Now there was a famine in the days of David for three years, year after year; and David inquired of the LORD. The LORD said, "There is bloodguilt on Saul and on his house, because he put the Gibeonites to death." [2] So the king called the Gibeonites and spoke to them. (Now the Gibeonites were not of the people of Israel, but of the remnant of the Amorites; although the people of Israel had sworn to spare them, Saul had tried to wipe them out in his zeal for the people of Israel and Judah.)[3] David said to the Gibeonites, "What shall I do for you? How shall I make expiation, that you may bless the heritage of the LORD?" [4] The Gibeonites said to him, "It is not a matter of silver or gold between us and Saul or his house; neither is it for us to put anyone to death in Israel." He said, "What do you say that I should do for you?" [5] They said to the king, "The man who consumed us and planned to

destroy us, so that we should have no place in all the territory of Israel— [6] let seven of his sons be handed over to us, and we will impale them before the LORD at Gibeon on the mountain of the LORD." The king said, "I will hand them over."

[7] But the king spared Mephibosheth, the son of Saul's son Jonathan, because of the oath of the LORD that was between them, between David and Jonathan son of Saul. [8] The king took the two sons of Rizpah daughter of Aiah, whom she bore to Saul, Armoni and Mephibosheth; and the five sons of Merab daughter of Saul, whom she bore to Adriel son of Barzillai the Meholathite; [9] he gave them into the hands of the Gibeonites, and they impaled them on the mountain before the LORD. The seven of them perished together. They were put to death in the first days of harvest, at the beginning of barley harvest.

[10] Then Rizpah the daughter of Aiah took sackcloth, and spread it on a rock for herself, from the beginning of harvest until rain fell on them from the heavens; she did not allow the birds of the air to come on the bodies by day, or the wild animals by night. [11] When David was told what Rizpah daughter of Aiah, the concubine of Saul, had done, [12] David went and took the bones of Saul and the bones of his son Jonathan from the people of Jabesh-gilead, who had stolen them from the public square of Beth-shan, where the Philistines had hung them up, on the day the Philistines killed Saul on Gilboa. [13] He brought up from there the bones of Saul and the bones of his son Jonathan; and they gathered the bones of those who had been impaled. [14] They buried the bones of Saul and of his son Jonathan in the land of Benjamin in Zela, in the tomb of his father Kish; they did all that the king commanded. After that, God heeded supplications for the land.

Part II

RESPONSES TO TRAUMA

THE STORY FROM 2 Sam 21 has many layers to ponder and to peel like an onion, often with tears. We will explore each layer through the lens of the experience of various people in the story, each lens giving a different flavor to the story, revealing different dynamics related to trauma.

As we peel back the layers of this ancient story we will explore a series of varying responses people have to trauma. After looking at each biblical character's response we will invite the reader to apply contemporary analysis and consider similar experiences.

These responses include:

1. The experiences of victims who survive trauma but get stuck in the traumatic experience;

2. Those for whom a traumatic experience becomes the driving force for defensiveness that gets expressed in aggression and actions that can create new traumatic experiences for others;

3. Those who transform the traumatic experience and move toward something constructive, perhaps even to reconciliation. This last exploration will be very complex as we look not only at the trauma survivor who transforms, but also at the offender who is transformed by what happens, and even raise questions of where God is—and isn't—in the story.

So let's dig deep, peeling through the story layer by layer!

3

THE VICTIM/SURVIVOR RESPONSE
Merab's Story

Merab: The Victim/Survivor

THERE ARE MANY VICTIMS in this story. The seven sons and grandsons of Saul were victims who did not survive. Five of the victims are unnamed, the sons of Merab, Saul's grandsons. Two of the victims were sons of Saul, and they are named: Armoni and Mephibosheth (there is a second Mephibosheth named in the story, the son of Jonathan, Saul's son and David's closest friend—this second Mephibosheth is spared because of David's love for Jonathan and the oath they swore about friendship being extended to their descendants [see 1 Sam 20:42]).

We can, however, assume with some confidence that these seven boys or men were all too young to have participated in Saul's act of genocide against the Gibeonites. King Saul died in battle at Mount Gilboa against the Philistines. Three of Saul's sons also perished in the battle, and they are referred to collectively as "Saul and his sons" (you may read the story of the Battle at Mount Gilboa in 1 Sam 31:1–13). All of Saul's sons old enough to be warriors, such as Jonathan, would have likely been with him and slain in that catastrophic battle.

So these young men, perhaps even some of them quite young since they included grandsons of Saul, were innocent of the crimes of Saul. They were scapegoats, convenient targets since the true author of the crimes was dead and thus beyond any worldly justice. In the story these seven die with no voices to protest their innocence. They were killed in a gruesome and humiliating way, impaled on stakes in a public place and their corpses left as carrion for the birds and dogs. The violence in this Bible story is definitely R-rated!

Our concern is for the victims who survive. We start with one of the mothers of the slaughtered seven, Merab. Merab was the daughter of King Saul who had ruled Israel before David. She was also the wife of Adriel. She bore Adriel's five sons. Her sons were all slaughtered at the request of the Gibeonites and the order of King David, impaled and literally hung out to dry.

What was her experience? The text is silent. She is a victim who is named then disappears.

When we do training sessions with this story after participants have grappled with the text for forty-five minutes we invite one of them to step forward as Merab, to act as this grieving mother in a role-play interview. We have had some amazing interviews given by "Merab" over the years, but one particular interview was the most powerful and most accurate to the text: "Merab" was silent.

The volunteer was Sari Saptorini, a young seminary professor from Indonesia. Sari noticed that Merab didn't speak in the text, so she decided not to speak in the interview. Instead, she gave physical and facial expression to a powerful concoction of emotions, so gripping that as we watched the interview being carried out by a colleague of ours we worried that the story had triggered some unknown older trauma in Sari leading to an emotional meltdown. As our colleague interviewed her, Sari/Merab seemed on the verge of explosive tears as her body collapsed in on itself. Getting no response, the facilitator asked if she could express herself with a piece of paper. Sari violently smashed the paper together then ripped it apart. She vehemently flung the tatters to the floor. Her body language expressed silent rage, seething inside yet helpless to act. Like Merab, Sari was silent, but Sari gave dramatic expression to the feelings that may well have been churning inside this mortified mother. As soon as the role-play interview was finished Sari burst into a smile that relieved our anxious hearts. She was acting in a dynamic and evocative way; in her silence, she captured the intense clash of emotions that must have been roiling within Merab.

The mother of the slain sons, Merab, lives, but no voice is recorded from her. In Scripture, she disappears from the story. Surely she had feelings, powerful feelings, perhaps like those captured by Sari. But in the text, Marab's feelings are unnamed and hidden. Surely she cried, perhaps in private, fearful that those who slaughtered her children might come after her. Perhaps she was numbed with the shock of the violence, sudden and jarring in its ferocity. Perhaps she was in denial about the impact of the calamitous loss of all her sons who were necessary for her well-being in a socioeconomic context where a woman depended for her livelihood on the status and provision of her male relatives. We don't know what she felt, but we can empathize with her as a human being. However, in the story, Merab is simply named and then fades into oblivion.

Merab is like so many victims of too many wars and acts of violence. The news and history narratives rush on to the next momentous events, but the victims who survive are silent. Sometimes they are named, sometimes numbered, but usually, they fade from view and memory—like Merab in this story. They may be forgotten, but they are not gone. These victims may be with us in our families, in our neighborhoods, and in our religious congregations. What is hidden in the silence?

The Victim/Survivor Cycle

The model we will explore is the "Trauma Healing Journey: Breaking the Cycles."[1] The model has three parts: The "Victim/Survivor

---

1. © 2004, Eastern Mennonite University, adapted from a model by Olga Botcharova. The authors have chosen to use an earlier version of the model, and an updated model can be found at emu.edu/star.

Cycle," the "Aggressor/Offender Cycle," and "The Trauma Healing Journey: Breaking the Cycles."

The Victim/Survivor Cycle begins with the "traumatic event or act of aggression." We can imagine the sickening feeling Merab must have felt as she took in the news; perhaps she was even right there watching her beloved sons being slaughtered. Ida Glaser describes such trauma as "an experience that combines extreme danger with utter helplessness."[2] Certainly that was Merab's experience.

Trauma is universally felt in the body and the emotions. Besides whatever physical damage there might be to the survivor of trauma, there is immediate neurological impact as adrenaline rushes through the body and brain. The human brain is wired for survival. The amygdala in the brain is particularly designed to detect threat and ignites an urgent response to fight, flight, or freeze. If the intensity of the neural survival pathways aren't quickly discharged they can remain stuck, causing various symptoms years after the traumatic event.

Next comes the emotional response: shock, denial, hurt, shame, and fear. Often there are tears and the searing questions: "Why me?! How can this be?! Where are my children?! *Where*

2. Glaser, "Trauma Observed," 54–55.

are they?!" Denial may be experienced in thoughts or words: "I must be dreaming. I'll wake up, and everything will be fine." Or the temptation may be to numb out such intense feelings. Some people "disassociate" emotionally and have a very difficult time being present or maintaining relationships in a healthy manner. Others who have been traumatized victims may turn to drugs, alcohol, or anything that can relieve the pain.

Intense feelings of anger and panic may rise up with the urge to strike out with fists, or stomp in rage, to destroy anything in sight. The anger can be turned toward God: "Why God, why has this happened to me?" Anger can also be turned inward. Depression can become debilitating, even life threatening, when contempt for the aggressor turns inward, morphing into self-contempt.

Fight, flight—or just freeze. Such powerful feelings can overwhelm a person and be suppressed out of a need to gain some sense of control. Glaser shared her own experience in which she spoke of it as trying "to convince ourselves that we are not really helpless."[3]

Merab was so vulnerable. Her sons would have been her only source of economic survival. Saul was gone and the relationship with David seems troubled, if we look at related Scriptures in 2 Samuel. It seems that she has no voice and gives no voice to her feelings in the Bible.

In the Victim/Survivor Cycle "suppression of feeling" leads to "ongoing feelings of shame and humiliation." A mother is supposed to keep her children safe and know where they are at all times. Merab failed, or so she may have felt. She failed to keep her sons alive, and the shame of failure might have shut her down. How could she ever again appear in public? Everyone knew her loss, and the shame of being left alone in society must have been unbearable. Without family she may have also experienced "loss of meaning" and purpose. During family celebrations she has no family with whom to celebrate; instead she is left with an empty table and a broken heart.

---

3. Glaser, "Trauma Observed," 56.

"Loss of meaning and a sense of helplessness" can intensify and spill over into other areas of life, robbing a person of the potential to thrive and grow emotionally and spiritually. Truly life comes to a halt, and there is a feeling of being stuck or pushed aside as life goes on for others.

For some people, not for all, there is a growing "desire for justice and vindication." The mind may become preoccupied with "fantasies of revenge," letting a desire to get even play out vividly in one's thoughts. If the mind goes down this road, there may come a new act of aggression that takes us into the next cycle: The Aggressor/Offender Cycle.

However, we don't see Merab move toward aggression, or at least the report of such is not in the text. People can indeed continue to move back and spiral around inside the Victim/Survivor Cycle. They never transition to aggression, and they never heal. People are all around us who are stuck in trauma, grief, bitterness, and pain, perhaps with physiological issues, illness, and disease taking their toll.

Time doesn't necessarily heal these wounds. Dan once met an elderly couple. The husband was in tears and couldn't speak. His wife related the story. In World War II he had been held as a prisoner-of-war by the Japanese army. He was horribly mistreated and tortured. After the war he suppressed all the feelings he had about his massive trauma. He got married, had a family and a career. He retired, and with age he just got tired of expending all the energy to bottle up his trauma deep, deep within. These powerful emotions began to erupt in a constant flow of tears. The wounds of this veteran were finally coming to the surface fifty years after the war.

Merab, whatever became of you? How many other walking wounded are there just like you?[4]

4. Trauma may be more than a personal or social experience but also an intergenerational one. Dr. Rachel Yehuda has found evidence of genetic transference of trauma. Major trauma can change genes in very specific and measurable ways, passing down the traumatic impact to children and even further generations. Thus, massive traumas such as the Holocaust or slavery can traumatically impact those who never had that direct experience. The Victim/Survivor Cycle goes on and on. See Yehuda, "How Trauma"; and Blades, "Trauma From Slavery."

4

THE AGGRESSOR/OFFENDER RESPONSE

The Gibeonites's Story

The Gibeonites: The Aggressor/Offenders

IN THE 2 SAM 21 story the Gibeonites are victims of trauma, suffering action that we would call genocide today. The survivors lived in the shame and humiliation of that awful experience until the opportunity came for them to exact revenge upon the descendants of Saul, the one who slaughtered so many of their people. The Gibeonites turned the tables from being victim/survivors to becoming aggressor/offenders.

Who were the Gibeonites? The first mention of them in history is in Josh 9 during the story of the conquest of Canaan by the Israelites. They came from the small city of Gibeon, just a little north of Jerusalem, as well as some surrounding towns. They were likely part of a larger ethnic group in Canaan called the Hivites who appear on the repeated lists of the people in Canaan the Israelites were to destroy (see Exod 3:17, among many references). The Israelites had utterly destroyed Jericho and Ai. Many of the Canaanite kings mobilized for battle, including most of the Hivites (Josh 9:1–2). Rather than wage war to protect themselves, the Gibeonites developed an elaborate ruse to sue for peace. They sent a delegation with donkeys loaded with old cracked wineskins and worn-out sacks. The delegates wore shabby sandals and tattered clothing. They carried dry and moldy bread.

When they met the Israelites they claimed to have come from a long way. At the beginning of the trip their clothes, equipment, and rations were new. Their rags and stale bread was all that was left after their epic journey. They told the tale of being sent on this long journey to ask for peace, and Joshua believed them. A treaty was made between Israel and the Gibeonites allowing them to live. Interestingly the Joshua text says the Israelites "did not ask direction from the Lord" (Josh 9:14). The treaty was sworn with an oath.

It only took a few days for the Israelites to realize they had been duped. The Israelites were furious with their leaders for falling for the trick. Joshua summoned the Gibeonites to explain themselves. After he heard their fears and feeling bound by the sworn oath of the peace treaty, Joshua agreed to let them live on the condition that they would be marginalized people among the Israelites. They would be bound to service as "hewers of wood and drawers of water" (Josh 9:23), menial tasks that would keep them impoverished but alive. Their service was specially designed to serve the worship of Israel's God, "for the congregation and for the altar of the Lord, to continue to this day, in the place that he should choose" (Josh 9:27). So they lived for a few generations without mention in any of the historical records.

However, as the Promised Land was apportioned among the tribes of Israel, the tribe of Benjamin was given the territory around the Gibeonites. About a century and a half after the conquest, Israel's first king was chosen, Saul from the tribe of Benjamin. In the 1 Samuel account of Saul, nothing is mentioned of the Gibeonites, though 1 Chr 9:35 places Saul's great-grandfather in the town of Gibeon. The city comes up in 2 Samuel as the site of two incidents during the seven-year-long civil war to determine who would rule after Saul's death in battle. However, the original people in that area are invisible and not heard from in the biblical narratives. Yet there must have been some sort of social intimacy for people sharing the same geographical space, though with one group clearly in the margins.

After David wins the civil war and the throne of Israel we have this incident recorded in 2 Sam 21 with no specific time frame. Israel is struck by a famine that lasts three years. King David prays, and God speaks, "There is bloodguilt on Saul and on his house, because he put the Gibeonites to death" (2 Sam 21:1). Later the text says in a parenthetical note about the Gibeonites that Saul "had tried to wipe them out in his zeal for the people of Israel and Judah" (2 Sam 21:2).

This is the only report we have of what happened to the Gibeonites. Today we would call it ethnic cleansing. Saul is described as having zeal for his nation, though perhaps it was more intimate and tribal as the Gibeonites lived among the Benjaminites, Saul's people. Military action was taken, and countless Gibeonites were killed. They lived in their silent victimhood for many years until the famine struck Israel. Then God spoke to David about this outstanding guilt on the land because of the gross violation of the peace covenant between Israel and the Gibeonites.

In response to this new awareness, David had the Gibeonite leaders come to him to determine what steps should be taken to set things right. David used the term "expiation" ("atonement" in some versions), a religious term for setting things right or removing sin and guilt from people. The response of the Gibeonites indicated they had no rights either to demand compensation or to ask for someone to be put to death. Perhaps David had initially offered financial compensation, and this was their polite refusal so as to move the discussion to more extreme solutions. David pressed the conversation further asking for their desires. The immediate response was for blood. The Gibeonites spoke about their trauma, how they "have no place in all the territory," but also with an intensity about Saul who "consumed" them and "planned to destroy us" (some versions say more intensely "plotted").

The Gibeonites ask for seven of Saul's male descendants to be handed over to them to be put death. Part of the punishment would be to expose the bodies to the elements and to the dogs and carrion birds to be eaten, a huge expression of shame upon the victims and their community. Furthermore, the Gibeonites say this act should be a religious one, "before the Lord," done in Gibeon. Ancient Hebrew texts give a variation that may be intentionally sarcastic referring to "Gibeah of Saul, the chosen of the Lord" (2 Sam 21:6).[1] The spirit of self-righteous vengeance is very strong in their statement. Though Saul had been God's "chosen" king, now his descendants would be sacrificially slaughtered to make atonement or expiation with God.

David concurs with the Gibeonites suggestion with one reservation. He requires that Jonathan's crippled son Mephibosheth be spared, harkening back to the oath between Jonathan and David (1 Sam 20). Their deep friendship would extend to their descendants. Mephibosheth is spared, but the other seven male descendants of Saul are handed over, the five sons of Merab, grandsons of Saul, and the two sons of Rizpah and Saul.

These seven young men—perhaps some of them were even children—were rounded up by David and his men. They were handed over to the Gibeonites who impaled them on stakes and left their bodies to be shamefully devoured and to dry out in the sun. Their action was a religious one, done on a hill held as a sacred space. The text says it was done "before the Lord" (2 Sam 21:9). The Gibeonites fade from the story, seemingly placated by this action that decimated the descendants of the man who had committed genocide against them. It's the end of the story from the Gibeonites' point of view. Justice has been served.

The Aggressor/Offender Cycle

The Aggressor/Offender Cycle[2] picks up where the Victim/Survivor Cycle ends but spins off into a new cycle with a different ending, namely an "act of aggression, committed in the name of

1. The alternative reading is in a footnote in the NRSV.

2. © 2004, Eastern Mennonite University, adapted from a model by Olga Botcharova. The authors have chosen to use an earlier version of the model, and an updated model can be found at emu.edu/star.

self-defense, and/or justice and restoring honor." The Aggressor/ Offender Cycle describes the process of moving through various stages from a sense of identity as a victim of trauma to justification of continued acts of aggression.

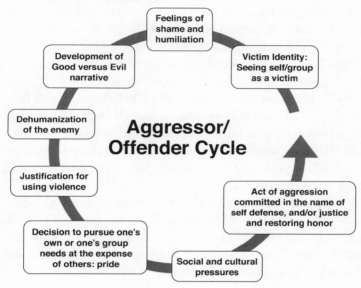

Saul, as King, broke a treaty with the Gibeonites. The result was genocide, creating personal and social trauma beyond imagination. The Gibeonites felt they had a right to be angry and seek revenge. King David gave them the perfect opportunity to do so. They didn't want money; they wanted the lifeblood of those related to King Saul. As victims, they were solid in their "victim identity." As a people group, they had never gained the upper hand over the house of Saul. Their feelings of "shame and humiliation" festered generating their trauma story. As a people, they felt profound shame in relation to other people groups, affecting their status in the international and interethnic political reality of their day.

There are at least two sides to every story. In the Gibeonite version of the story, Saul is the evil king, and, of course, the Gibeonites see themselves as innocent victims of a broken treaty. In the Aggressor/Offender Cycle, this is understood as the "development of the good versus evil" narrative. By labeling others as evil the victim can regenerate a sense of humanity and dignity that they felt robbed of by the offender.

The problem with this labeling is that the victim's identity continues to be defined by the trauma, and healing is not possible. Victim identity is so insidious because the act of aggression and the after effects of the aggression profoundly threaten the very core of how we see ourselves and how we see our group. The assumption is that the injustice of the trauma changes everything, and there is no way to erase it from history, no way to erase it from the hearts and souls of those affected. Only a truly evil person or superpower could do such a thing to us, the "good ones." "We are victims." It is a reactive stance, one that tries to make sense of the trauma. It is a reactive stance that seeks to restore some measure of pride and self-worth.

Modern examples abound, but one in particular is most illustrative. In 1999 the United States was mobilizing NATO (the North Atlantic Treaty Organization) to go to war with Serbia. In that context *Newsweek* magazine's April 19 issue had a dramatic cover. The bold, all-caps headline proclaimed: THE FACE OF EVIL. The photo was the face of Serbian President Slobodan Milošović with churning flames behind him, not so subtly evocative of the devil and hell. So one might ask, Who are the good guys? Of course, those mobilizing against this evil: the United States and NATO.

In Christian theology there are two opposing aspects of our humanity that make us the complex creatures we are. One is in the Creation account in Gen 1:26 where God speaks of making humanity "in our image." Every human being has the image of God stamped upon one's very being, however broken, shattered, or marred that image may be. The innate goodness is there. On the other hand the Apostle Paul writes in Rom 3:23 about humanity, " . . . since all have sinned and fall short of the glory of God." So there is also that of evil in us all. We each have that mix of good and evil, the face of God and the face of evil. When we engage in creating the "good versus evil" narrative we take a theological cleaver to our mixed humanity. The face of evil label is put on my enemy, which back in 1999 was Slobodan Miložović. We then assign to ourselves the face of God, which gives divine underpinning and blessing for whatever we do as the rest of the Aggressor/Offender Cycle spins around in its destructive course.

The next step toward justification for violence is "dehumanization of the enemy." If the enemy is hopelessly and intrinsically evil, then, of course, the enemy must be punished or even destroyed. There are words in every language that dehumanize the "other." Many such words reduce the human to an animal. Or worse, the words and descriptions further degenerate into "scum" or "garbage," something that doesn't even have life and is in fact rotten or despicable.

Political art is used in almost every culture and every conflict to depict the enemy as less than human or monstrous. Sam Keen's book *Faces of the Enemy: Reflections of the Hostile Imagination* explores the use of political art in the way the "enemy" is created, made evil, then dehumanized. It is hard to kill another human being, but if we can find a way to make that "other" into vermin or some sort of twisted, monstrous being, then the violence becomes acceptable, even heroic and positive in ridding the world of that evil.

Dan had an experience in which he witnessed the reversal of a "good versus evil" narrative. In February 2006 he was in Tuzla, Bosnia, in the wake of the terrible war that took place in the former Yugoslavia. The warring parties were ethnic Serbs, ethnic Croats, and Bosnian Muslims. An important fact in this story is that the Turks of the Ottoman Empire invaded the area in 1463. Conflicts along religious and ethnic lines continued to run deep and tragically were never resolved.

Dan was invited to do some conflict transformation training with a unique group: Protestant ethnic Serbian citizens of Bosnia, mostly women, meeting along with Bosnian Muslim male army veterans who were in a post-traumatic stress support group. There was an "aha!" moment in the training as they examined the Rizpah story and came to the Aggressor/Offender Cycle. One of the army veterans suddenly exclaimed, "Now I understand why the Serbs call us 'Turks'! I am not a Turk!" He realized that the enemy who had traumatized him had viewed him as a Bosnian Muslim through the lens of that historic invasion of the Ottoman Turks that profoundly threatened those of the Christian faith centuries earlier. His own "good versus evil" narrative disintegrated as he realized how that narrative had worked in his enemy's consciousness. Name-calling is evidence of how we project the pain and anger of our own trauma onto the other, the enemy. (We will come back to this story in the next chapter about the Trauma Healing Cycle.)

The Aggressor/Offender Cycle moves even closer to a new act of aggression when the decision is made to "pursue one's own or one's group needs at the expense of others." The good and evil story develops a "justification for violence." Eventually that justification moves toward creating a violent strategy. A plan emerges. It no longer matters that others may be hurt and that violence will create new victims. The enemy deserves to suffer. This is the opportunity that the Gibeonites had when David came to them. David was trying to assuage the bloodguilt of the former genocide committed by Saul and stop the famine in his kingdom. But this plan would only spill more blood on the land and the famine would not end. Violence brings on more violence, more trauma, and no healing in sight. The Gibeonites did not care. They deserved justice, and the "social and cultural pressures" were intense, encouraging their resolve for revenge. They even had the blessing of David to carry out their longings. Sweet revenge!

The Aggressor/Offender Cycle generates a "new act of aggression, committed in the name of self-defense, and/or justice, and restoring honor." The Gibeonites could once again hold their heads high. For decades they had been "hewers of wood and drawers of water," second-class citizens stuck in King Saul's oppressive system, climaxed by a genocide that heaped horrific injury upon insult. Now they could restore their former glory with the blessing of King David. Their violent acts to restore themselves left new victims and new traumas. The cycles of trauma and harm just repeat themselves again and again and again and again with new victims, some of whom will dream of their opportunity to become new aggressors. Is there any hope for breaking out of these cycles?

5

TRANSFORMING TRAUMA

Rizpah's Story

Rizpah: The Transformer

LET'S GO BACK THROUGH the story but this time put Rizpah in the center of our attention. Who is Rizpah?

Rizpah is identified as "the concubine of Saul," to whom she bore two sons, Armoni and Mephibosheth (same name but different person from Jonathan's son). Interestingly she is identified three times not in relation to Saul but as the "daughter of Aiah." We know nothing of Aiah other than that he was Rizpah's father. Yet having her identity as daughter of Aiah, stated repeatedly, likely has a purpose in the story, one hard for us to grasp at a distance. There is one other Aiah mentioned in the Bible, a clan leader descended from Esau (Gen 36:24 and 1 Chr 1:40). It may be that Rizpah is not an Israelite but a descendant from Esau. She certainly was not a wife in Saul's royal household, but merely a concubine, a slave bought or captured to sexually satisfy her king without the privileges of a wife.

What we learn about Rizpah is that she was a person from the margins. She was marginal in the house of Saul, a slave, perhaps from outside of Israel, a woman. She did have some status because of her sons who could be given royal privilege and even be in line for the kingship. However, once the house of Saul collapsed with Saul's death in battle and the loss of the ensuing civil war with David, Rizpah is even more in the margin. She has lost whatever prestige she might have had as Saul's dynasty has collapsed. Then with the execution of her sons, Rizpah is pushed even further to the margins with all her future security and livelihood lost with her children. Rizpah is an ultimate marginalized person with no power by any of the measurements of society. Yet she acts in a way that transforms everything.

Rizpah is a victim/survivor like Merab. She loses her two sons in a sudden and brutal act of violence. But she doesn't get caught up in the Victim/Survivor Cycle. Rather the first thing Rizpah does is to mourn. She grieves publicly. She comes to that public high place where the seven descendants of Saul including her sons were executed. She takes sackcloth, the traditional garb of mourning, and spreads it out on the ground to mark her place of vigil. She must have wailed over the bodies. She gives the torrent of her feelings full expression.

Rizpah also keeps the birds and other animals away from the bodies of the slain. This could be seen as just trying to protect the dignity of her sons and nephews in death, but there is more to this action. She is engaged in an act of civil disobedience, standing between the king and the full execution of his sentence. Part of the humiliation of this death was the desecration of the bodies by letting the birds and dogs eat them like carrion. We see this practice in many stories in the Bible, including in the stories of Saul and David. David taunted Goliath that his body would become food for the birds and wild animals (1 Sam 17:44–46). Then Saul was killed in battle at Mt. Gilboa along with all his sons old enough to be warriors. The Philistines took the bodies of Saul and his sons and nailed them to the wall of the city of Beth-shan. Letting the animals dispose of the carcasses was a sign of their utter humiliation. But the men of Jabesh-gilead from Israel slipped up to the city wall of Beth-shan. They took down the bodies of Saul and Jonathan and the other slain sons of Saul. They carried their bodies back to their own village and buried them there.

This dishonoring of the dead is part of the judgment against them. Such dishonoring is seen in the death of Queen Jezebel. She was thrown out of an upper palace window, and the dogs ate her body leaving her no burial place (2 Kgs 9:30–37). Rizpah cannot bring her two sons back to life, but she can maintain their honor even in death. So she stands vigil, driving away the vultures and ravens that would peck at her beloved children. She drives away the dogs and wild animals that come to scavenge. Her action isn't just one of love, but one of defiance against the orders of shame being allowed to come to their humiliating conclusion.

How long did Rizpah's vigil take place? There is only one verse (v. 10) given to her action, but it has a time frame: "From the beginning of harvest (specified in v. 9 as the barley harvest) until rain fell on them from the heavens . . . by day . . . by night." The rains did not come down immediately after the killing of the sons of Saul as a divine end to the drought-driven famine. Days and nights passed. Rather, v. 14 seems to indicate that the healing of the land didn't happen until after the bodies were buried at the end of the story.

So how long might this vigil have gone on? Most commentators identify the beginning of the barley harvest as April. The rains tended to come in the autumn. So imagine this vigil going on for months: April, May, and into June. What has happened to the bodies? Without the animals to eat the flesh, the bodies are drying out and decaying in the sun and wind. Soon they are mere bones becoming ever more bleached. Rizpah sees this. Her vigil will not bring these bones back to life. The dead are dead and will remain so. But Rizpah stays: June, July, and on into August. Through the heat of the summer Rizpah remains. What do people think of her? Do they plead with her to come home like Merab? It's time to get on with her life. Maybe people ignore her as they go about their business. She becomes a fixture, but you can look the other way as you go by. Maybe people call her "crazy." Maybe she was, but we think not. We think she was staying there, demanding that attention must be given to this atrocity. Just as the genocide against the Gibeonites went unrecognized for decades until God became the advocate for them, Rizpah refuses to let the murder of her children be forgotten. She is the sole advocate in this lonely vigil, the only one who will not give in to fear.

Finally, after long months—August, September, October—something happens. David hears about Rizpah's vigil. Interestingly David does not go directly to Rizpah. Instead, he goes to Jabesh-gilead whose villagers had rescued the bodies of Saul and Jonathan and the other warrior sons and kept them there. David exhumes their bones from their temporary graves and brings them to Rizpah. Why? In the wake of the dynastic war between the House of Saul and the House of David, nothing had been done to heal the rift. David comes with these bones that had never rested in peace and presents them to the mother whose sons he had ordered to be executed. It's a strange meeting. No details are told about it, but what an encounter! After all these months the killer is coming to the survivor with a peace offering. This is done in public. The king comes humbly before the grieving mother. Together, David and Rizpah then bury all the bones in the ancestral tombs. The bones are laid to rest with honor rather than exposed in dishonor. David seems dramatically changed in response to Rizpah's action. The conclusion to the story comes in v. 14: "After that, God heeded supplications for the land."

As we've gone through this story more slowly with Rizpah at the center, many details emerge. We will gain more clarity as we explore some of the theories related to the trauma-healing journey. Even deeper textures of the text emerge as we look more carefully at David's experience and at the role of God in the story. We'll unpack these step by step so the full richness of Rizpah's transformative action can be recognized.

The Trauma Healing Journey: Breaking the Cycles

We now examine the Trauma Healing Journey: Breaking the Cycle model[1] with Rizpah as the central actor. Rizpah is a victim and suffers trauma as a victim/survivor. In the story we see all the stages of that cycle, but now she is memorializing her grief in public witness, keeping the dogs and birds away from the bodies of her sons in the place of public execution. She has refused to stay stuck in victim mode. She also refuses to pursue a violent reaction. Her choice of action is to grieve in public. She doesn't seem to target King David in particular. Of course, we don't have a personal journal or record of her feelings, but we see she is distraught and she is not violent. She is mourning. This is the first action of breaking free and choosing to live, as painful as it is. She is "mourning and memorializing."

The next stage listed in the model is to "accept loss" and to "name/confront fears." This does not mean that the injustice of the loss is acceptable, rather one is in touch with the reality of the loss. Merab seems absent, perhaps in denial or hiding in shame. Rizpah, however, can be seen as one who is out in public with the enormity of her loss.

In the Trauma Healing Journey there is a questioning of "Why them?" In other words, the aggressor becomes humanized, and the victims realize that shortcomings in one's own group or system contributed to the violence and trauma. Who would know better the shortcomings of the dynasty and the political structure than a mere concubine? People in the margins are often acutely aware of the failures and weaknesses of the mainstream. People in the mainstream typically have blind spots, but margins must be aware to simply survive. Rizpah brings her marginalized self into the story as she grieves her loss. She no doubt knows that her actions can cost her life as she publicly defies the king's execution of her sons. But what does she have to lose? David has disgraced her;

---

1. © 2004, Eastern Mennonite University, adapted from a model by Olga Botcharova. The authors have chosen to use an earlier version of the model, and an updated model can be found at emu.edu/star.

he has broken trust with her and Merab and all women like them. She knows the root causes of the problem only too well, and now she has nothing left to lose. This leads to a commitment to take the risk of being cast out even further.

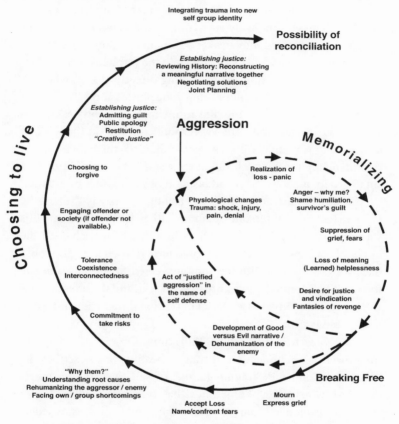

Trauma Healing Journey: Breaking the Cycles

In the previous chapter we told of Dan's encounter with a traumatized Bosnian Muslim army veteran who had been on the receiving end of Serbs who dehumanized him, referring to him as a Turk, connecting him to the Ottomans who invaded and ruled the region for centuries. "I'm not a Turk!" he proclaimed. However, as he studied with the group this story from 2 Sam 21 he burst out, "Now I understand the Serbs." Instead of seeing them only through the lens of his own trauma, he now could see their aggression as having grown out of the Serbian experiences with historic trauma. Serbs were no longer dehumanized enemies but rather people with a story of suffering that awakened his compassion. That Bosnian Muslim army vet's compassionate view of the ones who had traumatized him awakened an amazing response from a Serbian woman who had lost so much in the war herself. She asked if she could pray for him. Then looking directly at Dan who was facilitating she said, "I'm not asking your permission!" Turning to the Bosnian vet and looking him in the face she gently said, "I'm asking your permission." The vet responded, "Yes." In the wake of a shattering war that still sees people divided, the experience of rehumanizing the enemy brought a measure of reconciliation to a small group of people who had been on opposite sides of the war.

The next part of the Trauma Healing Journey is "Tolerance, Co-Existence and Interconnectedness." Rizpah did not initiate this stage; rather, King David did when he came to Rizpah with the bones of Saul and Jonathan. She could have refused him. She could have clawed his face with her long neglected fingernails. But she did not. She accepted his gesture of good will, and the offender and victim are now joined in a project of putting things right as best as they possibly can.

Ida Glaser, in her article "A Trauma Observed," addresses the power of re-connection in trauma healing. She describes the "disconnection" and "fragmentation" of self that trauma exerts on those who suffer.[2] Sometimes that fragmentation is deeper and more prolonged than anyone might notice or acknowledge. Therein lies the danger of failing to connect with God and others.

The journey through trauma literally demands "putting one's life back together," integrating the story with a different awareness and story of one's self after the trauma. As Rizpah expresses her grief and encounters David she is a changed woman. She connects to David through her trauma, and we have the text in 2 Sam 21 to prove it. Glaser states, "The memory matters. It is also the way in

2. Glaser, "Trauma Observed," 71.

which future generations, like us, can receive its blessing; the pass-ing on of the story gives it a significance for all time which makes the whole experience worthwhile."[3]

Upon meeting, Rizpah and King David act together to give proper burial to all the unburied bones of the House of Saul, in-cluding Rizpah's sons. We don't have a record of the conversation, but there must have been some words of engagement that were offered and received, as noted in the Trauma Healing Journey, "Engaging the Offender." All restorative justice models require this encounter between victim and offender in some form.

What about "Choosing to Forgive?" We don't know if Rizpah was able to forgive but she did set aside her grief for a moment to go with David and bury her son's bones. This was the moment of creative tension and creative justice in the story, as noted in the Trauma Healing Journey. This moment required thought and planning on King David's part: Admitting guilt and making a form of restitution to Rizpah.

Forgiveness is a complicated matter because we live in time and we hold memory. Sharon's personal definition of forgiveness is "being willing to bear the pain and hurt another has caused be-cause one values the relationship." There may not be any physical presence or relationship with the offender due to separation or death. But there is always an emotional relationship, carried in the victim's wounded heart. In this definition when memory arises, one is reminded that the relationship with the offender cannot change while one holds on to pain. One learns to carry the pain in a way that still gives room for the relationship. There is a time to confront and there is a time to let it be. Sometimes this means not harping on the pain or dredging it up in conversation, no matter how difficult that may be. Sometimes it means being willing to carry the pain in an emotional backpack instead of as an infection coursing through every cell of one's body. It means setting the pain in an emotional space that allows the relationship a chance to be healed. It doesn't make the pain less important or painful; it just

---

3. Glaser, "Trauma Observed," 72.

has a different weight and space for the sake of the relationship.[4] Rizpah seems to have done this. She left her deep pain at the execution ground and walked with David to the place of restitution.

From this point of the story we can only guess what the relationship between Rizpah and David is going forward. But we do know that the tribe of Benjamin (Saul's tribe) and the tribe of Judah (David's tribe) came together in future conflict during the civil war after the reign of Solomon (see chapter 6 for a more detailed discussion).

4. Stephen Cherry's *Healing Agony* explores a wide range of human experiences with forgiveness within the complexities of personal histories, relationships, and varying degrees of commitment to restitution, healing, and restoration.

6

DAVID

Hope for the Aggressor/Offender

David's Story through the Trauma Lens

WHAT ABOUT DAVID IN this story? He is obviously a major dramatic figure in the history of Israel and in these biblical texts. However, let's examine David through the lens of trauma. Was David ever traumatized?

David faced threats such as the lions and bears when he was a shepherd and then the mighty Philistine warrior Goliath when he was still a lad. Later David himself became a warrior and was involved in combat. Such experiences can produce trauma, but no indication of trauma is given in the particular texts.

Scripture records a more intimate relationship for David, in which trauma is very clearly experienced. After David's victory over Goliath, he was brought into Saul's royal household. There he became best friends with Saul's eldest son Jonathan and married Saul's younger daughter Michal. David went on various military forays, all of them successful, which led to Saul becoming jealous of David. Their relationship soured as Saul's mental condition began to deteriorate. Once when David was playing the lyre to try to calm Saul, the king hurled a spear at David but missed. Saul sent soldiers to seize David, but Michal helped David escape.

David turned to his former enemies, the Philistines, for refuge. When the Philistines turned on him David pretended he was insane. He drooled and scratched at doorways with his fingernails, so David was chased away like a madman. Soon David was out in the wilderness, living on the run. He gathered a band of other misfits and outcasts around him surviving by plunder and extortion. Twice Saul led expeditions to track David down. Twice David had the opportunity to kill Saul but chose not to, calling Saul "the Lord's anointed" (1 Sam 24:6). Eventually, David hired himself and his band to the Philistines as mercenaries, though being careful never to attack Israel. Meanwhile back at the palace Saul basically divorced Michal from David and gave her to a man named Paltiel to be her husband (1 Sam 25:44).

What was the effect of all this upon David's psyche? No clear psychological evaluation is given, but there may be a window into his soul when Saul and Jonathan are killed by the Philistines at the battle of Mount Gilboa. David is told of their deaths, and he immediately composes a poignant elegy: "How the mighty have fallen . . ." (2 Sam 1:19–27). His love and grief are expressed with poetic elegance: "O daughters of Israel, weep over Saul." But the bodies of Saul and Jonathan and the other warrior sons of Saul had been nailed to the wall of a Philistine city. David, the mighty warrior who slew Goliath and gathered two hundred Philistine foreskins as the bride-price for Michal, did nothing. He sang a beautiful song, but he left the bodies of both Saul and even his dear friend Jonathan hanging in shame. He left the burial tasks to the men of Jabesh-gilead.

David acted much like the son of an abusive father, someone with a love-hate relationship. Saul had adopted David into the royal family. He married David to his daughter. But Saul also abused him, trying to pin him to the wall with a spear and later hunting him down in the wilderness. David's own experience of trauma seems to set the stage for deep inner conflict, perhaps first revealed in the contradictory responses to Saul and Jonathan's deaths at Mt. Gilboa.

David then appears to become the victim/survivor who morphs into the aggressor/offender, at least in relation to the house of Saul. The seven-year civil war for control of the throne leads to David's triumph and the deaths of Saul's heir Ishbaal and his commander Abner. Jonathan's maimed son Mephibosheth poses no threat to the throne, but there are seven other male descendants of Saul who could make a claim to the throne. When the historic moment arrived with the famine and the need to make things right with the Gibeonites, those with a mind for hard-nosed politics would see this as a gift-wrapped opportunity for David to continue the purge of the House of Saul. David quickly agreed to the Gibeonites's proposal and handed Saul's seven sons over to be slaughtered. David's trauma seems to be melded with political expediency to shed blood as an aggressor/offender himself.

Can an aggressor/offender find the way back to healing? The Gibeonites fade from the story. Whether the blood sacrifice of Saul's descendants made them feel that the score for the genocide was settled or that they had uneasy feelings for the blood now on their hands, nothing is said in the text. Some offenders have no desire to set things right.

David, however, takes a different path. David seems comfortably ensconced in his palace, thinking the matter between the Gibeonites and the House of Saul is concluded, though evidently the drought and famine continued. Then David hears about Rizpah. Something in her action changes David. He likely had known Rizpah personally. His own hardness toward the House of Saul may have numbed him to the horror of what he was doing in signing the death warrants of those seven young men. From the text, it appears that Rizpah awakens something deep in his heart. She speaks of humanity: Her humanity, the humanity of her dead children, and David's own humanity. This was a horrible intentional tragedy.

Some Christians reading this story think that David has to be the hero. Most of the Bible commentaries interpret the story as one where David responds appropriately to God's labeling of bloodguilt on the house of Saul (more on that in the next chapter!) by giving the seven male descendants to the Gibeonites for slaughter.[1] David is simply moved by Rizpah's grief and acts in compassion toward the grieving mother. Such an interpretation, however, misses a number of key elements to the story including the emotional intensity of the trauma that comes with such a violent violation. David can't just "make nice" to comfort this grieving mother. He's one of the killers! His comfort would not be welcome!

This is where the details of the story become very important. When David hears about Rizpah's action he doesn't go straight to visit her. Instead, he goes to the village of Jabesh-gilead where the bones of Saul, Jonathan, and the other warrior sons of Saul had been kept. This was a raw wound still ripping across Israel, a legacy of the seven-year-long civil war. David was the victor, and the House of Saul was left in defeated shame. David gathers all those bones and comes with them into the presence of Rizpah. This action is out in public. The killer comes to the mother of the victims, but he brings the bones of the rest of the family who had not been allowed to truly rest in peace. David cannot bring back the dead, but he can restore honor to the house of Saul, honor he had personally either ignored (as in not rescuing the bones of Saul and Jonathan) or deliberately sullied (in allowing the Gibeonites to slaughter the seven male descendants and leave their bodies exposed as carrion). Now he comes in a humble posture to this angry, grieving mother with what seems to be a peace offering. He brings these bones to show his positive intention to Rizpah. It appears in the story that David didn't do the right thing before, but he intends to do so now.

From this point on the action is plural, David and Rizpah act together. They gather the bones of all those slain. Together they bury the bones in the ancestral lands, in the tomb of Saul's father Kish in the tribal lands of Benjamin. Now those slain can truly rest

---

1. For example, see Youngblood, *1 & 2 Samuel*, 1056; Bergen, *1, 2 Samuel*, 446; Keil and Delitzsch, *Biblical Commentary*, 462–63; Baldwin, *1 & 2 Samuel*, 284–85; Arnold, *1 & 2 Samuel*, 620; Thompson, *Penitence and Sacrifice*, 115.

both in peace and in honor. Is there also an act of forgiveness of some sort from Rizpah that allows David to rest in peace? Perhaps, though no word of forgiveness is spoken in the text. David had certainly seen the awful toll taken by this long conflict between the two dynastic houses. The texts give indications that the conflict raged into David's own heart, and it certainly spilled out to mar the lives of others. David's change of action is a key element to the drama. David moved past participating in the violence to restoring honor through the proper burying of the bones.

David is not presented as a pure, pious saint in the biblical texts. There are two major stories of sin David committed that had huge public impact. The best known is the story of his adultery with Bathsheba (perhaps not adultery between consenting adults but sexual exploitation by the most powerful man in the society) followed up with his plotting the death of her husband Uriah (2 Sam 11 and 12). The second story is the census of the people that was actually a form of draft registration because the goal was to find out how many men were available for military service. This was a move away from trusting God to trusting the centralized military might the king could control (2 Sam 24 and 1 Chr 21). In both cases David was confronted by a prophet, first Nathan and then Gad, in his wrongdoing. In both cases David repented, a powerful expression of which is found in Ps 51. This story in 2 Sam 21 may be the third of the big stories of David's sins. He wasn't morally in the right in having the sons of Saul killed. Rather he compounded the sin of Saul's genocide with the wrongful killing of innocents to even the score. Instead of Nathan or Gad as the prophetic presence to confront David, the text presents Rizpah, the grieving mother. Her dramatic vigil over her dead sons is as vividly compelling as Nathan's parable of the lamb taken by the wealthy man leading to his confrontation with David, "You are the man!" (2 Sam 12:7). As in the two better-known stories, the story with Rizpah reveals the pattern of David responding positively when faced with the damage of his sin. He can't undo what has been done, but he can seek to make things as right as possible.

There is a bigger healing that goes beyond the fourteen verses of this text. A deep division existed between the house of Saul and the house of David and between their respective tribes of Benjamin and Judah. Samuel anointed David as king following the death of Saul and the heir-apparent Jonathan. David fought and killed Ishbaal, Saul's next surviving son and Abner, Saul's military commander. David from the tribe of Judah triumphed. Saul's dynasty was overthrown, putting the tribe of Benjamin on the losing side. This story of the annihilation of the male descendants of Saul (except the maimed son of Jonathan) takes us to the bitter bottom of that division.

Fast forward through the history of Israel. David dies, and his son Solomon becomes king. Forty years later Solomon dies, and civil war once again tears apart Israel. Only one tribe stays with the dynastic line of David, namely the Tribe of Benjamin, Saul's tribe (1 Kgs 12:21). How was the deep rift between these tribes bridged? There is no story about mending the division between the Houses of Saul and David, between the Tribes of Benjamin and Judah, except this strange and awful story in 2 Sam 21.[2] At the center of the story is a traumatized, marginalized woman, Rizpah, who takes sustained, nonviolent, courageous action. Her action brings about a change of heart in David, one of the aggressors in the story. Through David's action to gather all the bones of Saul and his sons and bury them properly and with honor, the deep rift is healed. Reconciliation takes place in a way that lasts for generations. Rizpah transforms the direction of Israel's history.

Hope for Aggressor/Offenders

Aggressor/offenders can stay stuck in cycles of revenge creating new victims. But this story plays out in a more transformative

2. There were some from the tribe of Benjamin who joined David's most intimate band of warriors when David was driven into the wilderness by King Saul, according to 1 Chr 12:2–7. Between David's ties to these "mighty warriors" and his profound personal relationship with Saul's son Jonathan, there were some links that could possibly have played a role in rebuilding the bonds between tribes and families.

drama. The Trauma Healing Journey process requires deep change to match the seriousness of the consequences of aggression and the trauma it produces. The focus of this discussion is about actions that intend to do harm, "justified" acts of aggression that flow from the "good and evil" narrative created by the aggressor, seen in the Aggressor/Offender Cycle.[3]

As an aggressor, the one who ordered the execution of Saul's seven sons, David appeared to be living through the Victim/Survivor Cycle in his conflicted relationship with Saul when Saul was alive. The pain of being pursued by Saul to within an inch of his life surely created times of helplessness and emotional injury in David that we see in the Victim/Survivor Cycle. The famine scenario and the conversation with the Gibeonites gave David the supposed justification to re-enact the trauma, creating new victims and more trauma, borne by Merab and Rizpah in the horrifying loss of their sons.

Rizpah's public grief that went on for a few months is the beginning of the transformative Trauma Healing Journey. She names her pain and loss, moving past denial to an acceptance that "this is real, and this is tragic!" Acceptance in this case is not acquiescence; it is accepting the fact that the pain one is feeling is real and naming the horror of it. Victims have difficult work to do!

In most cases, the moment of understanding the traumatic root causes of violent offensive acts comes through telling one's story, encountering the "other" in a safe or brave space, perhaps with a counselor or mediator. Both parties must be willing to risk encounter. One quality that makes David such a fascinating character is that he has a repentant heart. Whenever he understands that he has grieved the heart of God with his behavior he repents and seeks to be restored to the God he loves. We see this is in Ps 51 and other penitent psalms. In this story David appears to be moved by Rizpah's actions to reconsider his own part in her story. He realizes that God has not ended the famine and something

3. Moving past and beyond nonintentional traumas such as natural disasters, illness, and accidents are matters for other books. One of the best we have found is Rendon's *Upside*.

more must be required of him. So he engages this grieving mother and follows through with an act of repentance toward God and toward Rizpah.

What if the aggressor/offender is unwilling to engage? In this story the Gibeonites disappear after their act of retributive violence, never engaging as far as we can tell in a journey toward healing or reconciliation. Many aggressor/offenders never participate in an effort to face the consequences of their action or to bring healing to shattered relationships. In that case, victims can still reflect on the personal and corporate shortcomings apparent in the aggressor/enemy. Such reflection is key to moving through the victim's pain experienced in intentional violence. In the Trauma Healing Journey this is the "Why Them?" question. For the sake of one's own personal transformation, "victim identity" or brooding contempt is not a space that invites healing. Sometimes counselors will ask victims in a counseling session to speak to an empty chair that represents the offender. Journal writing or writing a letter (though it may never be delivered) are other possible ways to explore the root causes of the offender's actions. For the one who experienced the loss from violence, choosing to forgive[4] can be as much for the sake of one's personal peace of mind as it can be the path to reconciliation and restored relationship.

Breaking the cycle in the Trauma Healing Journey requires humility for the offender to accept that one's actions have created unintended consequences or consequences that may have seemed slight at the time of the offense. If Rizpah had not raised her voice, would King David have ever reflected on what he had done and how it affected these two mothers? David had enough humility to consider his actions in a different light, and at some point he chose a course of action that brought him into connection with Rizpah. The burial of the bones of Saul, Jonathan, and the seven sons of Saul was a public act, in essence, an apology for leaving them out

---

4. Stephen Cherry speaks about the difference and sometimes needed option of having a "forgiving heart" instead of actually extending forgiveness because of the complexities of situations of violence and lack of access to the offenders (*Healing Agony*, 100–102).

in the sun to be ravaged by birds and dogs. David could not bring back the dead, so the next best possible restitution was to give a proper burial and acknowledge the pain in Rizpah's heart. He was willing to engage Rizpah, and together they buried the bones.

We know that the "establishing justice" part of the cycle was realized because the famine ended! Scripture records that when David finished the burial of the bones, with Rizpah, God restored the crops to the land. We know nothing of how Rizpah and David related to one another after this ritual of burial. But we do know that Rizpah was courageous and fearless in her memorializing of her loss. We also know David publicly came to Rizpah, the mother of the ones he ordered killed, and he acted to restore the dignity and honor to the House of Saul that he had helped strip away through his actions. There the story ends, and anything we might speculate about their later relationship only comes from imagination.

In the Aggressor/Offender Cycle a narrative is developed of "good versus evil," with, of course, the aggressor who had been wronged before being the one who is "good" and thus justified in whatever action is taken against "those evil enemies." As victims, if we dehumanize people in our version of a trauma story we don't give the offender an opportunity to change. Upon seeing King David, Rizpah could have beaten him with her fists or tried to kill him in her grief. Rather she accepted his offer of restitution and was open to breaking the cycle.

How does the narrative change in the journey toward healing and reconciliation? In the Trauma Healing Journey, the "good versus evil" narrative evolves in complexity. The story is not so much black and white; there are shades of gray, nuance, recognizing there is more to the story than was first realized. Every side has trauma and sadness, and every player in the story has a personal or social history related to violence. Rizpah can be viewed as the hero of the story for her nonviolent transformative action, but even she comes from a family that had been complicit in genocide.

For an aggressor/offender to come forward and break the cycle of violence requires personal courage and risk. This biblical story would have had a very different ending if David had avoided or been too fearful to look at his personal motives and actions. He had to ask himself, "What have I done here?" "Why has God not stopped the famine?" "What message does Rizpah have for me?" "Have I acted on faulty assumptions rather than justice?" David risked the personal reflection that led him to action, to meet Rizpah, and to bury the bones of her sons, of Merab's sons, and of Saul and Jonathan together. This was a very courageous action with historical impact, and it also involved risk on David's part, contextual political and spiritual risk. What if Rizpah, and also what if God, rejected David's attempt at making amends?

Perhaps David's conscience would not allow him to avoid this risk. Perhaps the Holy Spirit was speaking to him that he must follow through, igniting an urgency to correct his path and take a turn toward God's definition of justice.

We can reasonably imagine that after Rizpah and David met, she told the story to her neighbors and friends, and, most likely, she felt vindicated to some degree. David risked meeting this courageous woman. He did his best to make things as right as possible between himself and this grieving mother. He honored her sons with a decent burial. Now Rizpah and David could tell the same story, with an ending that brought healing to an entire nation. The Journey Toward Healing describes "reconstructing a meaningful narrative together" as a late step in the process toward reconciliation. Out of the horrifying incident of the slaughter of the descendants of Saul a new narrative emerged; we have the direct evidence of that new narrative in what is recorded in 2 Sam 21. It's not a simple story glorifying one side or the other. It is not a narrative of "good versus evil." Every character is complex. Both the House of Saul and the House of David could recognize this new complex narrative as true.

For aggressor/offenders and victim/survivors what are the conditions that promote the self-reflection, courage, and risk-taking necessary for the Trauma Healing Journey? In our day and time, what motivation and what support are needed to break out of old patterns? In the Scripture, King David is heralded as a "man after [God's] own heart" (see 1 Sam 13:14). Spiritual disciplines and maintaining a listening stance with God make peace more likely. These practices allow us to be ready for the encounter with the "other" that may bring about greater justice and peace. The capacity to engage in self-reflection and the humility to approach God and others are characteristics we see lifted up in the life of David. He is a model for us about how aggressor/offenders can change and be a part of breaking the cycles of violence, despair, and pain. Rizpah is a model for us about how persons living at the margins can raise their voice. God was at work through Rizpah; her voice was the key that unlocked David's heart to consider the story from new angles. An awful story in Scripture becomes a new story, a story of reconciliation. God is still at work today to break cycles of violence and their seemingly never-ending traumas.

7

WHERE IS GOD IN TRAUMA?

WHERE IS GOD IN trauma? Elie Wiesel in his play *The Trial of God* depicts questions raised of God in an Eastern European Jewish community in 1649 following a series of pogroms. The idea grew out of his own experience as a teenager in Auschwitz when one night in their barracks three Jewish scholars put God on trial for indifference to what they were suffering. The verdict wasn't exactly "guilty," but rather *chayav*, "He owes us something." After a long silence, the scholars and others present had their evening prayers.[1]

The question of "theodicy" is often wrenched out of agony in terrible experiences. Where is God? Is God responsible for this? Is God innocent? Is God guilty? Is God absent? Does God owe us something? The story in 2 Sam 21 is fascinating for where God is and where God isn't. This story provides one answer, a partial one, to the question of God amid human traumas.

God first appears at the beginning of the story. David prays about the famine going on in Israel. God speaks to David: "There is bloodguilt on Saul and on his house because he put the Gibeonites to death" (v. 1). There is the question then about God causing the famine, a question that is echoed in the frequent attributing of various disasters to God's judgment upon Israel or other nations

1. Frazer, "Wiesel."

for evils perpetrated (see Amos 4:6–13, for example). That major theological and ethical question is for another book to grapple with!

However, one thing is clear. The marginalized people who had been victims of genocide, namely the Gibeonites, had nobody to advocate for their cause. So in the story God became the advocate for these victims, even against God's own covenant people. This injustice would not be allowed to stand as business as usual. Since nobody from Israel raised the call for justice, God did. In this text God is the advocate on behalf of the victims. God speaks for and acts for those treated unjustly.

In the text God does not tell David what to do. God simply tells David what the problem is. The plan of action to kill the seven male descendants of Saul came as a result of David's discussions with the Gibeonites.

David and the Gibeonites carry out their acts of violence as religious action. The action from their point of view is carried out "before the Lord," stated repeatedly in v. 6 and v. 9. You could call this human sacrifice to atone for the violent misdeeds of Saul. However, though the act of execution was done "before the Lord," God is silent. There is no heavenly response, no blessing of the land, and no ending of the famine. It seems as though this supposed sacrifice is not well received by God.

This would not be the first time in the Bible that a sacrifice was not well received by God. Cain and Abel carried out the very first ritual sacrifices offered in the Bible, recorded in Gen 4. God accepted Abel's sacrifice but not Cain's. No explanation is given in the Genesis story, but Cain responds with the first act of violence, the murder of his brother. Other sacrifices are rejected in the prophetic writings. Amos cried out, "Even though you offer me your burnt offerings and grain offerings, I will not accept them; and the offerings of well-being of your fatted animals I will not look upon. . . . But let justice roll down like waters, and righteousness like an ever flowing stream" (Amos 5:22, 24). Isaiah proclaims God's word: "What to me is the multitude of your sacrifices? says the Lord. I have had enough of burnt offerings of rams and the fat of fed beasts; I do not delight in the blood of bulls, or of lambs, or of goats. . . . When you stretch out your hands, I will hide my eyes from you; even though you make many prayers, I will not listen; your hands are full of blood. Wash yourselves; make yourselves clean; remove the evil of your doings from before my eyes; cease to do evil, learn to do good; seek justice, rescue the oppressed, defend the orphan; plead for the widow" (Isa 1:11, 15–18). Just because an action is done in God's name or as a ritual to placate God doesn't mean that it is blessed or condoned by God. So the silence of God rather than the claims of the Gibeonites tells us about the moral dimensions of this act. The sacrifice of these seven descendants of Saul is *not* accepted by God.

Cephas T. A. Tushima in his book *The Fate of Saul's Progeny in the Reign of David* posits that David actually violated the law in two specific ways in the killing of these seven sons of Saul.[2] First, the killing of Saul's descendants for Saul's own crimes violates the Deuteronomic Code. Deut 24:16 declares definitively, "Parents[3] shall not be put to death for their children, nor shall children be put to death for their parents; only for their own crimes may persons be put to death." This theme of each person being responsible for their own sins is seen in passages such as 2 Kgs 14:5–6; Jer 31:29–30; and Ezek 18:2–4. We know these seven who were executed were innocent of the genocide. If they had been old enough to participate they would have been with Saul at the disastrous Battle of Mt. Gilboa. But these were younger children at that time or perhaps not even born yet as Merab's children were Saul's grandchildren. David broke God's law in turning over innocent children to be killed for their father and grandfather's crimes.

Desecration of corpses by leaving them to rot in the weather or to be eaten by carrion is also outside Israel's law and practice. Deut 21:22–23 specifically orders that people executed for capital offenses be taken down and buried on the same day. To leave the bodies exposed without proper burial actually desecrates and

2. Tushima, *Fate of Saul's Progeny*, 214–15, 221–22.

3. "Fathers" in the literal translation from the Hebrew and is used in most older English translations.

defiles the land. Joshua deliberately followed the Deuteronomic Code in how he dealt with the corpses of the executed Canaanite kings, burying them before the end of the day (see Josh 8:29 and 10:26–27). So David's action with the Gibeonites in exposing the bodies of Saul's descendants further defiled the land, rather than removing the bloodguilt.

Though the execution of these seven sons was done as a religious act, God is silent. God doesn't accept the human sacrifice of these young ones for the sins of Saul. The famine goes on. The land is still defiled, even more so.

The second and last time God appears in the story is at the very end. After David and Rizpah together bury the bones of Saul and all his slain sons in the ancestral tomb, the text says, in various translations: "After that, God answered prayer on behalf of the land" (New International Version); "After that, God heeded supplications for the land" (New Revised Standard Version); "After that, God took pity on the country" (Jerusalem Bible); "Only after that was God prevailed on to show mercy to the land" (Complete Jewish Bible); "And God answered prayers to bless the land" (Contemporary English Version). The prayer that David offered in v. 1 is only answered in full when David's behavior has changed in response to Rizpah's transformative action.

The merciful response of God to one who confesses and repents of wrongdoing is seen in David's soul-baring psalms. In Ps 32:5–6 he says, "Then I acknowledged my sin to you, and I did not hide my iniquity; I said, 'I will confess my transgressions to the Lord,' and you forgave the guilt of my sin. Therefore let all who are faithful offer prayer to you; at a time of distress, the rush of mighty waters shall not reach them." In Ps 51 David sang, "For I know my transgressions, and my sin is ever before me. . . . Deliver me from bloodshed, O God, O God of my salvation, and my tongue will sing aloud of your deliverance. . . . The sacrifice acceptable to God is a broken spirit; a broken and contrite heart, O God, you will not despise. . . . then you will delight in right sacrifices" (Ps 51:3, 14, 17, 19a).

Where is God in this story of trauma? God is not in the religious blessing of violence. Rather God is the advocate of the victims of violence. God speaks for those who have been ultimately marginalized by injustice. God also responds to changed hearts resulting in changed behavior. When the victim and offender negotiate the path to healing and reconciliation, then God's healing spreads to the wider circle, to "the land."

8

TRANSFORMING TRAUMA
The Present and Future Journey

MANY OF THE STORYLINES we hear about trauma focus on the new things we are learning about PTSD, post-traumatic stress disorder. Wars of the twentieth century had terms for this condition, such as shell shock and battle fatigue. Our society has definitely made a lot of progress in understanding the nature of such conditions and in developing empathy and support for those who have experienced trauma. There is a temptation, however, to sympathetically focus so much on the impact of the trauma that we ignore human resiliency. We trace the story of the Merabs of the world through their trauma into their shattered victimhood, exploring and enumerating all the dimensions of their condition. We see the survivors of the trauma as damaged goods.

Rizpah reveals that being stuck in victimhood isn't the only possible story arc for someone who experiences major trauma. She acted and became a shaper of her own story and destiny, impacting others. We don't get an intimate glimpse into her psychological or emotional processes; we just know of her actions and the impact of those actions on David and the long-term relationship between David and Saul's tribes. Obviously, something profound happened within Rizpah. After all the events were over she likely didn't sink back into just being a victim of the trauma. Rizpah had reshaped the entire narrative around her, which likely was reflected in her own inner reshaping about how the story of the trauma was integrated into her sense of who she was and what her life meant.

Jim Rendon addresses this longer story arc of people who have been through trauma in his book *Upside: The New Science of Post-Traumatic Growth*. Rendon explores how trauma is a dividing line in people's lives, but not necessarily one that leaves people broken and irreparably damaged. For many people, the trauma propels them toward transformation, dealing both with a deeper understanding of who they are and what they are about as persons, but also inspiring personal action to make the world, or at least a slice of it, better. The traumas involved great suffering, but for many people that suffering was a catalyst that led to finding new meaning for their lives. Many studies of people who have gone through major traumatic events showed that over half of them reported positive changes in their lives as a result. How can that be?

For a traumatic event to lead to growth, it must shake people to the core. What was assumed and accepted is shattered. Within that shattering is an opportunity to get outside the box of the previous life and put together a new sense of meaning about oneself and one's vocation in life. This is not a quick process; rather it can take many years. But it is a deep journey, going to the very depths of how a person sees oneself and understands one's place in the world. Rachel Yehuda, Director of the Traumatic Stress Studies Division at Mount Sinai School of Medicine, summed up the different way of assessing the impact of trauma: "You do recover in some ways, but that recovery doesn't actually involve returning to the baseline. It involves recalibration towards something new, and PTSD is a way of describing that in a very negative light, and post-traumatic growth is a way of describing that in a very positive light."[1]

---

1. Rendon, *Upside*, 59–60.

Rendon presents six essential tools for growth. First is telling a new story,[2] something we've seen in unpacking the Rizpah story. A traumatic event can shred the old narratives people or societies have about themselves, shattering worldviews and undercutting any sense of meaning. To grow through the trauma a new story needs to be developed that incorporates the traumatic event but in a way that makes it the starting point for a new and better way of being oneself. For this story to be reworked, an individual needs to take an intentional step of engaging in "deliberate rumination,"[3] an activity not driven by the trauma but driven by the survivor moving toward transformation. The trauma is no longer "in control"; but rather the person who experienced the trauma takes control of shaping meaning and the future course of action. This is a transformative and liberating step.

Rendon's second tool for growth is relying on others.[4] Community and support are vital for change. In one study of combat veterans returning from the Persian Gulf War, social support was the number one predictor for whether a person grew from their trauma or not. The kind of support that is most effective is that which allows the trauma survivor to dictate their needs, which helps in recovering a sense of autonomy and becoming the driver of the healing process. In the story in 2 Sam 21 Rizpah seems to act alone. But community builds as her action brings David into the healing process. As they bury the bones of Saul and his slain sons and grandsons it is likely that a larger community began to come around them, possibly including Merab as well. In the stories that follow in this book, many involve a community of survivors with similar stories who support one another as well as outside friends who encourage and give hope.

Expressing oneself is the third tool, particularly honest communication.[5] Allowing, encouraging, and supporting a person to talk about the trauma can enable the deliberate rumination to

2. Rendon, *Upside*, 69–75.

3. Rendon, *Upside*, 78.

4. Rendon, *Upside*, 87–93.

5. Rendon, *Upside*, 108–12.

occur. It assists bottled up emotions to come out so they can be processed. Many professional therapists, and even just family and friends, have helped in this process by encouraging survivors to tell their story, to perhaps draw or journal or find some expressive channel to bring out the emotions related to the trauma. In simply expressing those emotions a reflective process begins to happen whether consciously or unconsciously. Rizpah didn't have the support of counselors, but she gave public vent to her emotions. What she thought about as she kept vigil alone for months by the bones of her children is impossible to say, but she seemed to be the only one who was honest about what had happened.

Rendon's fourth tool is looking for the positive.[6] He sees a transformative power in optimism. This is not a thin weak optimism, but a positivity that deals directly with what happened and how one will move into the future. Framing an event positively or negatively makes a huge difference in how one processes it. This is not to say that whatever happened in the trauma was good, but rather to focus on what was beneficial in coming out of the experience, even in a very small way. The loss is real and profound, but noticing and expecting positive outcomes can help in engaging the trauma in a transformative way.

Questions of meaning quickly lead to matters of faith, which Rendon sets forth as the fifth tool.[7] There is a religious path to growth for many who transform their traumas. Almost all religions incorporate stories of trauma, struggle, and transformation. Setting one's own story in this meta-story of faith provides a context for supporting hope. The religious stories teach about suffering, but also that suffering does not have the final word for how we shape our meaning or our actions. Often this faith journey is a difficult one with questions directed at God or the divine. How could God let this happen to me? The Rizpah story is full of questions about where God is and where God isn't in the terrible events that unfolded. Was God in the killing of Rizpah and Merab's sons, an act carried out with religious ceremony? The rejection of

6. Rendon, *Upside*, 127–32.

7. Rendon, *Upside*, 142–46.

this religious understanding is seen in the way the narrative in 2 Sam 21 reveals God's silence in relation to religious violence and only healing the land when Rizpah's action transforms the heart of one of the perpetrators of that violence. The biblical text doesn't answer all the questions and may even prompt more questions. For Rendon the faith journey is an important part of the healing journey. He writes: "Those who view their lives and the trauma through the lens of religious faith will likely struggle with their understanding of their religion—their framework for understanding how the world works and how they should lead their lives. Then they will have to move forward, using deliberate rumination, narrative reframing, and other tools to build a new and often deeper sense of faith and spirituality."[8] We don't get an intimate window into Rizpah's own faith, but we see this spiritual and theological reframing in the text coming out of Israel's faith community.

The final tool Rendon offers is opening up to new experiences.[9] Creativity spurs change and drives growth. Instead of personal paralysis, having worked through the trauma brings an honest openness to the future and the possibilities it holds. Rizpah's actions changed David, prompting him to act "outside the box" of his own earlier politics regarding the house of Saul. When he came to Rizpah with the bones of Saul and the sons killed at Mt. Gilboa, Rizpah and David together acted in a new way that laid to rest not just the old bones but also the old animosities. They acted in a way that couldn't have been predicted, a way that transformed the relationship between their tribes for generations to come.

Rendon helps us see that trauma is not a life sentence to victimhood. There is an upside that can be realized through honesty, hard work, and faith. He anchors his points in the stories of many survivors of trauma: maimed war veterans, survivors of debilitating accidents, and people stricken with life-threatening illness. He unpacks their stories of how personal trauma became a catalyst for personal transformation. Many of the survivors found new meaning in helping others face the same kinds of struggles they

8. Rendon, *Upside*, 147.
9. Rendon, *Upside*, 165–68.

went through. It is important to recognize and celebrate these triumphs over severe adversity; otherwise our shared understanding of trauma will be stunted and not fully supportive of the resiliency in these survivors.

Yet there is another dimension in the Rizpah story beyond personal survival and transformation. Rizpah takes us to an "upside" beyond that which is laid out in Rendon's book. Rizpah didn't just grow through her traumatic experience. She changed the entire context that had spawned the violence that claimed her sons and traumatized her. Whatever was going on inside her, Rizpah's actions were public and had a public impact.[10] Her actions had a powerful social and political upside. Rizpah changed the course of history in ancient Israel! She is not the only trauma survivor to have an impact on the social and political world that traumatized her. She has many "daughters" who have followed in her footsteps in their own unique settings and moments of history. We now turn to their stories.

10. Ida Glaser writes about how she now is beginning to think of her childhood trauma as "one of the best things that ever happened to me." Glaser goes further than the personal, however. She sees that her personal journey of trauma transformation has been more valuable than all her academic qualifications "for working on the Muslim-Christian interface in today's troubled world" ("Trauma Observed," 52–53). Her experience with trauma and trauma transformation has had a positive public impact in how she engages in her work.

Part III

DAUGHTERS OF RIZPAH

THE ANCIENT BIBLICAL STORY of Rizpah lifts up a traumatized marginalized woman who used nonviolent means to express herself and speak out to her society, resulting in transformative change. Rizpah is not the only example we see of such a woman taking transformative action. There are many examples of such people throughout history and most certainly in our contemporary era. We use the title Daughters of Rizpah to honor traumatized people, especially women, who marshal their own anguish, anger, and gifts to bring transformation.

In this section we tell stories of some of these Daughters of Rizpah. Most of them would have no knowledge or understanding of Rizpah at all, but they have acted much like she did in challenging the violence and injustice around them while standing—or marching—with their own loss and hope. They bring the archetypal dynamics found in Rizpah's story to life in many different national contexts and within the settings of a variety of conflicts. All these women experienced some great trauma or loss. Each one has a unique story, but each woman found her own path of transformative action. They all chose nonviolent methods. Some are Christian, some Muslim, some of no particular faith; yet all had a compelling moral compass and inner passion that allowed them to speak truth to the powers that be.

Some of these stories are well known. Leymah Gbowee was awarded the Nobel Peace Prize. Some of these women were featured in major news stories. Some are known only in smaller circles and are people we came to know through our own peacemaking travels. We personally know enough stories of other women from many different countries to fill two more books. So we chose these stories to be representative rather than in any way comprehensive or a ranking of the most important stories. The stories of these women have touched us personally in one way or another. What we hear in Rizpah's story echoes in their lives and actions. We invite you to let these Daughters of Rizpah speak to you today.

9

COMADRES OF EL SALVADOR

COMADRES IS THE ACRONYM in Spanish for the Committee of
Mothers and Relatives of Political Prisoners, Disappeared and
Assassinated of El Salvador. The COMADRES are most certainly
Daughters of Rizpah. As grieving mothers, daughters, and sisters
like Rizpah, they gave voice to those silenced by the death squads
in El Salvador. More than 80,000 people lost their lives between
1979 and 1992 in the civil war in El Salvador. The COMADRES
group was organized in 1977 at the urging of the Archbishop of
El Salvador, Monsignor Óscar Romero. Many women were encouraged to participate in organizing and political experience
through the church. They were active members of Christian "base"
communities in both rural and urban areas. These communities
studied the Bible through the lens of politics and social analysis
and learned about God's preferential treatment for the poor of this
world. The women were deeply involved in these communities,
and many remember the communities as the source of their political activism.[1]

Human rights activist Maria Teresa Tula was one of the
women whose faith was very important to her when she was going through imprisonment and torture. Monsignor Romero was

1. Tula, *Hear My Testimony*, 204.

a beacon of hope for the poor and oppressed in El Salvador. She treasured her times with him, reading Scripture and discussing the call to discipleship, and how to heal the community of injustice and oppression. Romero's love for and solidarity with the people gave ordinary people like Maria and the COMADRES a living example to follow. From him and their own faith, they gained profound hope and steadfast courage to take action.

The parallels to Rizpah can also be seen in the physical location of public grief. Rizpah mourned in public where her sons and the sons of Merab lay slain. The COMADRES' work took them to the most gruesome sites imaginable: unmarked graves and clandestine cemeteries. The mothers and relatives of people who had been imprisoned and murdered or disappeared by the government found each other during their search for the bodies of their loved ones in the jails or at the terrible cemeteries where mutilated bodies were dumped by the death squads. Maria accompanied these grieving women. Their numbers grew, and their passion for justice gained momentum as they searched together. These brave women of COMADRES faithfully and fearlessly denounced the human rights violations then and still do so today. Like Rizpah, they bore public witness in an undeniable venue and fashion.

Rizpah was a grieving mother. She had no husband as the concubine of the deceased King Saul. The loss of her sons affected her economic and social status and her ability to survive. Like Rizpah, at first Maria's actions grew out of her desire to protect her family because her husband was detained by the military. He was a trade union activist and ended up in jail. Initially she had no idea he was involved in social justice work. He didn't tell her because he was afraid she would turn him in to the authorities.

As time went on Maria gained more understanding of structural injustice, and she became motivated to confront the military and government about the gross violation of human rights in her country. Maria recognized her own oppression as a Salvadoran woman and went through many transformations. We don't know if Rizpah made these connections to structural injustice, but King David did. He was struggling with how to end the famine because of bloodguilt on the land. The political connections are always there in our personal stories. The COMADRES called those connections out and named them for the injustices they represented.

Maria joined COMADRES in 1978. These women refused to be silent. Their first public action was taking over a Salvadoran Red Cross building. Then they organized a hunger strike, followed by taking over the United Nations building in San Salvador. Like Rizpah, the women gained attention beyond their own personal grieving. They earned international attention through the 1980s, winning several peace and justice awards. Maria truly appreciated the moral and spiritual help she received from the women's group. Their work was important, but the support was also a source of hope for her because the work was dangerous. Many of the women personally experienced detention. Five were assassinated, and three were disappeared.[2] Rape played a huge role in the torture of these women. The trauma was compounded when some of the women who were raped were shunned by their husbands as damaged goods.

Maria's own marriage had to go through many changes. Eventually her husband was released from prison. Maria's activism often took her away from her husband, children, kitchen, and her "traditional" role in the family. At first her husband supported her work even though he had difficulty finding general employment after being a political prisoner. At one point he became very jealous of her work with the COMADRES, and they had a violent fight. They separated briefly, but eventually they worked it out.

Maria tells the harrowing story of one of the women named Sylvia Olan who was disappeared. This was a term used for abduction and torture by the military or police of activists or persons suspected to be activists, accompanied by official denial that the person had been detained. Olan had been the secretary of an electrical workers union and active in various strikes and actions against the government. The women found her body. She had been brutally raped, tortured, and maimed. To witness her battered body was a huge source of grief and fear for the COMADRES.

2. Tula, *Hear My Testimony*, 2–3.

In 1979, a coup brought in new leaders, the Revolutionary Government Junta of El Salvador, who promised peace and to resolve cases of disappeared persons. There was a lot of distrust between the people and the junta. The junta soon proved to be violent and oppressive of the people. The Rizpah story is uncomfortable for some to read because King David is described as a "man after [God's] own heart" (1 Sam 13:14). How can such a king do wrong or be criticized? The coup was supposed to replace a violent dictator and bring in justice and peace. The disappointment must have been profound and discouraging for both Rizpah and for the COMADRES.

The COMADRES took food and aid to political prisoners and helped families locate the bodies of loved ones who had been captured and tortured. Confrontations were provoked between the demonstrators and the Salvadoran soldiers in San Salvador. When soldiers began firing on the demonstrators, people ran into the Church of the Rosario, but the soldiers fired into the church, massacring many civilians who had sought refuge. The junta denied the existence of the mass graves or clandestine cemeteries, yet the COMADRES were discovering twenty-five to thirty bodies a day.

The conflict intensified when an assassin gunned down Monsignor Óscar Romero while he was leading the mass in the Rosario church on March 24, 1980. Shortly after Romero's death, Maria's husband was captured again. He was accused of terrorism and killed by the military. She had to look for his body and stumbled upon his family who had taken possession of the body for burial. From that point on everyone in her family was afraid to talk to her. She was unable to return to her home because it was not safe.

Maria became homeless with three children and one on the way. She went from friend to friend and place to place. Eventually she found a house near some relatives of her husband. She had nothing. She and her children slept on the floor and ate from one plate. Her oldest son went out to do construction work at age twelve. Maria was pregnant at the time and had a daughter born August 21, 1980. In the hospital there was no electricity. There were no sheets on the bed, and there were two women to each bed, along with their babies.

Meanwhile, COMADRES was constantly targeted as an organization. The COMADRES office was bombed in 1980. One morning they found three decapitated bodies in front of the main entrance to the building. The work of the COMADRES was very dangerous, but they were a force to be reckoned with and did not flinch while fighting for justice.

In 1984 the COMADRES increased the intensity of their public witness. They took to the streets proclaiming the "streets belong to the people not to the government and military."[3] They always wore black when they marched or protested. They increased their international visibility by visiting embassies and welcoming international journalists to document the atrocities they were experiencing daily.

As the human rights abuses increased, including the targeting of the women activists, Maria fled to Mexico. She needed time to grieve the loss of her husband and she was personally in danger. The authorities were constantly looking for her. She asked for political asylum in Mexico, but her request was denied.

The COMADRES had precious few victories along the way. As true Daughters of Rizpah, they were persistent and did not give in easily. Political prisoners were badly treated by the common criminals in the prisons, and their lives were threatened. This brutal treatment by other prisoners was a terrible experience, especially after being tortured by security forces on the way to their imprisonment. In spite of all the brutality they experienced, the COMADRES were able to organize political prisoners and secure for them separate quarters in some of the prisons. This was a hard-won victory in their struggle for justice.

The women had a very strong sense that they weren't just fighting for themselves but for social change in their country. They had a global view of what justice was all about. Maria wrote: "If there isn't drastic social change in our country then we will always be oppressed even if we win our rights as women. For us our

3. Tula, *Hear My Testimony*, 119.

struggle as women includes many things. I think it's fine for the women in the groups we meet to be talking about feminism and discussing the oppression that women have suffered for centuries. Everyone has the right to wage their struggles as they see fit."[4]

By 1985, after lots of international lobbying, there were still two thousand political prisoners in jails. Instead of "disappearing" people, the military were simply putting people from the opposition in jail.

Maria returned to El Salvador, but she was abducted on May 6, 1986 as she was on her way to the COMADRES office. She was tortured in prison and had another baby. Her six-year old daughter was also with her in the jail. President Duarte released Maria in a supposed humanitarian gesture following immense international pressure. But Duarte's action was pretty much a sham. During the televised release the president extended his hand to Maria, but she refused to shake his hand. Instead, she handed him a documented list of demands from the women in the jail!

After her release she was still in great danger so she fled again to Mexico. After traveling through Mexico Maria entered the United States by crossing the desert at night with a "coyote," a guide for persons seeking illegal entry to the United States. Maria applied for asylum and was initially denied. The immigration officials said she was a terrorist and a threat to US security. Even though she had letters from congressional leaders supporting her asylum claim, she could not get asylum for years. She was finally granted asylum in 1994.

In the United States Maria told her story as she traveled in the forty-eight mainland states. After awhile she declared there were no more tears when she would tell her story. "I always answer that I have to tell my story because the tortures we received in El Salvador were sent by the United States."[5] "I know from my own experience, the United States doesn't always defend democracy."[6] Even as she was seeking asylum in the United States Maria acted

4. Tula, *Hear My Testimony*, 125.
5. Tula, *Hear My Testimony*, 174.
6. Tula, *Hear My Testimony*, 175.

as a true Daughter of Rizpah. She was still unafraid to speak her truth to power.

Maria felt deeply ashamed that she had been raped during her torture. The shame of trauma also makes Maria in particular a daughter of Rizpah. It is ironic that such powerful women as Rizpah and Maria feel deep self-contempt and shame. It takes great emotional strength to reach inside and find worth when so many experiences in life knock you to the ground and crush you in the dust. Shame is part of the Victim/Survivor Cycle and can be debilitating and paralyzing. True Daughters of Rizpah get up out of the dust and keep on telling their story, making their grief known to bring about change for others. The act of giving voice puts shame in its place, demanding that one be seen and heard as a person of worth and deserving of justice.

During the 1990s COMADRES became more focused on equal gender roles and holding the state accountable for the education and political participation of women. Their idea of mothering became larger than just taking care of one's family but also including taking care of one's country and the rights of all people.

On December 31, 1991, the FMLN (the opposition military alliance) and the government agreed to sign peace accords in El Salvador. When Maria's testimony was written in 1991 her main concern was for human rights in El Salvador and for the government to punish the people who participated in the death squads. At the same time, Maria wanted to continue to work with the CO-MADRES to help build reconciliation in her country. She wrote, "We need new plans on how to help the wounded from both sides, whether they are government soldiers or soldiers from the FMLN who did not receive any medical help for years because of the conditions they lived in."[7] Dealing with her own direct experience with the government brutality, however, she wrote that she cannot forgive those who tortured her. "I don't feel hatred, but I have pain, a deep pain that will never, never be forgotten."[8] In the Trauma Healing Journey reconciliation is only possible when the hatred

7. Tula, *Hear My Testimony*, 185.
8. Tula, *Hear My Testimony*, 185.

turns to pain and you also see pain in the eyes of those who were the aggressors and offenders. Trauma gives birth to new trauma unless the enemy is humanized as one who also needs healing. Maria reached the point of seeing the needs of the wounded from both sides.

Lynn Stephen, the editor and translator of Tula's *Hear My Testimony*, speaks of women's testimonials integrating the personal with the political. Most stories begin with family relationships. In the case of Maria Tula, she had her consciousness raised through her husband's trade union activities. Her political motivation, like many of the women activists, came through the detention, disappearance, and assassination of a family member and sharing that suffering with other women. Like Rizpah, her political and public action grew from her personal pain and brought about amazing changes in an oppressive system.

Sociopolitical analysis and connection led these women to make new demands with a much broader scope: An end to incest, rape, and sexual harassment; providing land credit and technical assistance for women; stopping the rising costs of basic goods; equal opportunity for girls in school; respect for the environment; a better quality of life for women; development policies that take care of women's needs; laws that don't discriminate against women; and higher representation of women in positions of power in government. Women's testimonials create a "collective truth." "Stories of marginalization and oppression bind women together. Those giving testimony are sometimes not believed, but when testimonies are combined it is more difficult to deny the truth of the stories."[9] Testimonials and stories build solidarity with others who have experienced the same or similar oppression.

Through their experiences of personal suffering amid a context of massive systemic violence and their collective witness about the oppression, Maria Teresa Tula and all the COMADRES women are Daughters of Rizpah!

9. Tula, *Hear My Testimony*, 228–29.

10

THE NAGA MOTHERS OF INDIA

TWO HUNDRED YEARS AGO the Naga tribes in what is now northeast India and northwest Myanmar used to be headhunters. Intertribal and inter-village conflicts culminated in "taking heads" of the enemy. However, women played a role in restoring peace among the villages and tribes. Naga women today have mobilized to play a more structured and persistent role in seeking peace in larger conflicts. They have become advocates and voices of conscience amid long, bloody struggles. These women are Daughters of Rizpah.

Neidonuo Angami, along with other Naga women, formed the Naga Mothers Association (NMA) in 1984, initially to work against the rising social problems of drug addiction and alcoholism that were having a corrosive impact on Naga society. Angami's father was a government official who was assassinated by Naga insurgents when she was six years old. Raised in poverty by her mother, she experienced first-hand the hardships of social vulnerability. However, she persevered in getting her education, eventually becoming a teacher and social worker. When the NMA was formed, Angami became the founding general secretary, later serving as the organization's president, though she became popularly known as "the mother of peace."

The Nagas are a tribal people of Mongolian roots, which created a political identity crisis as India moved toward independence. The Naga National Council (NNC) participated in the struggle to throw the British out of India. On the eve of independence NNC leaders met with Mahatma Gandhi, saying they wanted to be independent as they didn't feel they were Indian. Gandhi said there would be no forced union, so on the day before India's Independence Day, the Nagas declared their independence. After Gandhi's assassination, Nehru refused to recognize Naga independence. The conflict eventually became violent in the mid-1950s leading to a war in which tens of thousands of people, if not far more, were killed. A flawed peace process in 1973 seemed to end the war but actually turned the conflict into a far more complex and difficult problem to solve.

Some key Naga freedom fighters rejected the peace accord, splitting off from the NNC. Then each of those groups splintered more with each faction claiming to be the true bearers of the Naga cause. By the late 1980s and early 1990s as many Nagas were being killed by other Nagas as Nagas were being killed by the Indian Army, something Neidonuo Angami had experienced directly with the assassination of her father.

As the conflict continued to spiral into increased violence, the Naga Mothers Association began to gather the bodies of the unclaimed dead. Sometimes they would go to the Indian Army bases to collect young Nagas killed in combat. In Naga culture, the dead were buried in newly woven shawls. Shawls are the primary Naga cultural garment, beautiful red and black blankets with other colors incorporated into patterns that identify the various Naga tribes. Weaving a shawl takes much work, and it is an act of love toward the dead person who would be buried in it. As the violence increased the Naga Mothers found themselves weaving as many as ten, twelve, or fifteen shawls a week for their young ones. Their exhausting labor of love led them to become more active in advocating for an end to the violence that produced so many dead. Like Rizpah it was the personal connection with the slain that moved them into the public space.

Angami and other leaders among the Mothers began to travel back and forth between the headquarters of the various insurgent groups and the Government of India calling for a cease-fire and political negotiations to end the conflict. Sometimes their trips took over a week, traveling on remote rutted dirt roads or taking boats on turbulent rivers, finally hiking into the jungle hideaways to meet with insurgent leaders. Then as they met with government leaders they pleaded as mothers to humanize the Naga fighters: "No matter what they are also freedom fighters, and our sons and brothers, and not terrorists."[1]

Besides calling for negotiations the NMA appealed to the Naga insurgents to stop recruiting children as part of their underground military units. They launched the "Shed No More Blood" campaign. Former Indian Home Secretary G. K. Pillai, who participated in the Indo-Naga peace talks, spoke about how this slogan was evocative of the pain felt by mothers who after bearing and rearing their children lose them to armed conflict.[2] This gave the Naga Mothers moral power as they spoke to both government and Naga insurgent leaders.

In 1997 the NMA played a key role in securing the first ceasefire between Naga militant groups and the Indian Army. Then when the peace talks stalled with the government of India the NMA joined with other Naga civic groups—churches, human rights organizations, student groups, and business organizations—in the Journey of Conscience.[3] Inspired by Gandhi's Salt March and the Freedom Rides in the US Civil Rights Movement, these groups took a publicized train ride from Nagaland to the Indian capital of Delhi. There they met with Indian civil society leaders to discuss peace, laid a wreath at Gandhi's tomb, and demonstrated in the streets for a just negotiated settlement to the Indo-Naga conflict.

1. "To End Bloodshed."
2. Wikipedia, "Naga Mothers Association."
3. Dan Buttry facilitated in the training and strategizing workshops that led to the Journey of Conscience actions. Ms. Angami presented that author with a Naga shawl. See Buttry, *Peace Warrior*, 73–76.

A number of times the Mothers thrust themselves into the middle of tense stand-offs between Indian and Naga forces. One Indian Army checkpoint in the state of Manipur, just south of the state of Nagaland and also with a large Naga population, had become particularly notorious for how Naga civilians were ill-treated. The NMA gathered at the checkpoint to demonstrate. Neingulo Krome of the Naga People's Movement for Human Rights had come to document what was going on. Indian soldiers seized Krome to keep him from publicizing the incident. A large group of unarmed women rushed toward the soldiers and wrestled Krome free. Then they stormed the barricade and tore it apart with their bare hands. The checkpoint was abandoned from that point on.[4]

In 2003 Mrs. Khesheli Chishi became the second president of the Naga Mothers Association. She continued the efforts for reconciliation and peace. During a particularly violent outbreak of the intra-Naga factional conflict, Chishi walked from Nagaland on the India side into the jungle headquarters in Myanmar to meet with S. S. Khaplang to urge him to back off from the violence and rejoin the reconciliation process. Reconciliation may have been an unintended consequence of Rizpah's action, but for the Naga Mothers, it was a major aim and driving objective. They became part of the Forum for Naga Reconciliation with that stated goal as their clarion call to Naga society as well as the various insurgent groups.[5]

As the years have gone by the NMA has become a major player in Naga civil society, providing leadership in social and political issues. All Naga women are considered members of the NMA and can become official members by paying a mere one rupee for dues (about two US cents). Abieu Meru, president of the NMA as of this writing following Mrs. Chishi in 2010, spoke about how all women are considered mothers in their context: "We called ourselves mothers because this name is apt for a woman here even if

4. This story was told to the authors in January 2005 shortly after it happened by a number of Naga Mothers and Neingulo Krome.

5. Dan Buttry participated in many of the mediations sessions convened by the FNR as told in Buttry, *Peace Warrior*, 206–14.

she has not borne a child. In Naga society, an aunt or an elder sister also has the same position as a mother. So a girl as she grows up is already a mother."[6]

As the political negotiations and reconciliation efforts have continued, the Naga Mothers have also continued to be active in putting out fires in the ups and downs of a process that doesn't seem to end. The NMA has broadened their scope to take on other issues, including the grip of patriarchy in Naga politics. They have mobilized with other women's groups for a major campaign to reserve 33 percent of legislative seats for women. Though they haven't succeeded yet, they have inspired many women to enter politics.

As this book headed into the editing phase the final agreement from a peace process between one of the Naga groups and the Government of India was about to be announced. Then the coronavirus erupted around the world, overwhelming many other political agendas, including the India-Naga talks. However, peace with the Nagas stirs up deep concern among neighboring states, particularly Manipur to the south where violence between Nagas in Manipur and Kukis and Meiteis has often flared with intense ferocity. The NMA has been completely locked out of the official peace negotiations, but with Manipur's growing turmoil the Naga women took the initiative into their own hands once again. They contacted the major Meitei women's organization in Manipur for extensive discussions about how to keep peace between their peoples. As one activist said, "It is as though the men will do the tough talking, but when it comes to doing the dirty work of frontline peace, it's the woman's job."[7]

The dual peace efforts of reconciliation among the various Naga factions and between the Nagas and the Indian Government have demanded a long-term commitment. The Naga Mothers Association has proven they have the leadership, vision, and passion to sustain such a struggle. Their voice is strong because they speak out of their love and sorrow as grieving mothers. Through their

6. Sinha, "Crusader on a New Battle."
7. Saikia, "Mothers of Nagaland."

determination they have forced powerful men to listen, whether high government officials or leaders of insurgent groups. They have been key leaders in the Naga civil society movement that has taken the initiative away from the guys with the guns and instead made reconciliation the driving demand of the Naga people for any who would claim to represent them. Neidonuo Angami, Khesheli Chishi, Abieu Meru, and all the Naga Mothers are Daughters of Rizpah!

11

MOTHERS OF THE PLAZA DE MAYO IN ARGENTINA

IN HIS FOREWORD TO *Circle of Love Over Death* by Matilde Mellibovsky, the Argentine writer and economist Antonio Elio Brailovsky pens an exquisite social analysis of the "Dirty War" (*guerra sucia*) of the 1970s in Argentina. About thirty thousand people disappeared. These people were targeted as political dissidents, Montoneros movement faction members, or left-wing Peronists. Students, labor union members, writers, and socialist-leaning militants were all suspect. From 1974 to 1983 the Argentine Anticommunist Alliance (AAA) operated right-wing death squads that kidnapped, tortured, and murdered anyone posing a threat to the neoliberal economic policies of the AAA. The death of such persons was justified by earlier violence, from 1969 to 1979, undertaken by the Montonero and ERP (People's Revolutionary Army). Brailovsky writes, "We would prefer to forget the horrors" of such a time, but "collective memory does not forget."[1] Even though many citizens enjoyed new levels of economic security and prosperity, there was that nagging memory that some people were no longer around to enjoy the Argentinian *belle epoque*. Due

1. Mellibovsky, *Circle of Love Over Death*, ii.

process for those kidnapped and disappeared was grossly absent, but the general population was apathetic and preferred to believe the government was beyond reproach in creating a new, prosperous society. Many people in Argentina felt that if their children were not targeted and the sirens passed by their house, then they could breathe a sigh of relief and simply go on with business as usual.

Long nights waiting for children and loved ones who never came home gave rise to other voices. Matilde Mellibovsky has documented them in *Circle of Love Over Death*, twenty years after the loss of tens of thousands. The Mothers of the Plaza de Mayo (Asociación Madres de Plaza de Mayo) are Daughters of Rizpah. Beginning in 1977, they risked their own lives to bring cultural trauma into public memory by remembering their children, by asking persistent questions about justice, and demanding to know what others preferred to ignore. Every Thursday until 1983 the Mothers kept vigil at the Plaza de Mayo in Buenos Aires in front of the Casa Rosada presidential palace. The Mothers kept "memory" alive, specifically the memory of their children, the closest they could come to see them alive again. Their white scarves were originally the diapers of their lost children, each embroidered with the child's name. They marched together, often carrying large photo posters of the missing ones, linking hearts and hands to speak out against the human rights atrocities of the government.

As victims of trauma, the Mothers of the Plaza de Mayo suffered so much. In their testimonies recorded in *Circle of Love Over Death*, the Mothers describe a wide range of feelings upon learning of the disappearance of their children: Feelings of horror, confusion, anguish, and fear. Many felt that time had stood still, and were tormented by the raging questions within: "How can life go on? How could people not care? Who ordered this? When will the pain stop?" Tragic grief made some of the women feel crazy, much like Rizpah, refusing to leave her place of vigil and shouting at the birds and dogs to leave her children whole. One Mother made a cake on her daughter's birthday and eventually put it under a tree, believing her daughter would find it there. Some Mothers literally could not eat, because normal activity felt like a betrayal of their child whom they could no longer see at the table. Some left an empty chair at the table just in case their child would arrive home for the meal, especially at holidays. Some kept looking for their children, talking aloud to them, and some felt premonitions of "presence" or death.

Trauma is felt in one's body. Marching around the plaza together, feet on the pavement, was a grounding ritual that allowed the women to express with their bodies the pain inside their souls.

Rizpah was not afraid to defy the king's business and put her body between the king and her dead sons as she kept her courageous vigil. The husbands of the Mothers were afraid of the very public action of their wives. Some of the women testified in the book that their stomach hurt every Thursday, so great was the fear of coming out in public to vigil. Sometimes the police would come out and harass the women. Upon reflection, the Mothers found these small and inconsequential encounters with the police actually gave them courage to be bolder. What more did they have to lose? The Mothers could have retreated into seclusion, but they chose to turn their anguish and suffering into the energy of a powerful movement for justice. Some of that power was the power of memory: "That is what gives life; memory nurtures the root from which life grows."[2] This poetic expression was what motivated the Mothers. The need to tell their story, to speak up, to give voice was an important part of healing from trauma. Their courage to do so was remarkable.

Rizpah also gave voice to her grief, though she appeared to be a lone actor. At least the Mothers supported each other and marched together week after week. Victims of trauma often feel alone and isolated. The bond of victimization and trauma brought the Mothers together. They defied isolation and forged connection. They held the belief that "your child is my child," and the temptation to be silent, to surrender to their own fears or the fears of their husbands and friends was a temptation they resisted as they marched together.

2. Mellibovsky, *Circle of Love Over Death*, xv.

The "Vigil Place" is also an important part of the story of Rizpah and for the Mothers. Obviously the bodies of her sons were a continual reminder of the horror of their execution in Rizpah's place of vigil. The Mothers of the Plaza de Mayo are named for their place of vigil. People came to expect to see them there every Thursday. Many went out of their way to avoid the place, fearful of being seen as a person in solidarity. But for the Mothers, the place of vigil came to be a haunt, a trigger for their grief. The plaza took on a new identity, no longer the entrance to the palace, but the gateway to the machine of death.

The vigil place cries out, *"Where is the body of my child?"* Mothers are supposed to know where their children are at all times. The "no place" of the disappeared was implied in the plaza as the vigil place. Having no place to lay the bodies of their children, the plaza became the cemetery of the absent ones. It was as close to the grave of their children as they could come.

What gives oppressive power the audacity to carry out such horrific violence? The government held an ideology of economic policy wedded with a brutal fixation on national security as they defined and controlled it. A huge amount of money was required to put these policies in place, to eradicate perceived threats to the economic goals of the elite and powerful. The government was not about to waste all that money, so they kidnapped, tortured, and murdered an entire generation who stood in their way. The government counted on the naiveté of the victims and their families. Grieving and traumatized people are sometimes slow or unable to act or advocate so the "powers that be" can take advantage of such profound emotional paralysis. In reality, however, oppressive powers rely on pillars of support that can be eroded by nonviolent persistent people power movements. Rizpah stepped forward with resolve, in spite of her profound grief, and her actions impacted the king. The Mothers articulated their grief but also made a space for creative response, showing their enormous capacity to break the silence, to counteract the complicity of the public at large. They were not naive. They possessed wisdom that everyone needed to stop the cycle of trauma and violence written into the script of

Argentine politics, from colonization to the militarization of various groups gaining power in cycles of trauma re-enacted again and again.

Nonviolent action is not a guarantee of protection. In the biblical story, Rizpah took a risk when she kept her public vigil, defying the dogs and the birds that would steal the flesh of her children. She could have been executed just like her sons for interfering with the king's business of public execution. He fully intended for the bodies to be left to public disgrace, but Rizpah's vigil demanded a response. David eventually came to Rizpah with a repentant heart and offered a proper burial for her sons. But Azucena Villaflor, the founder of the Mothers of the Plaza de Mayo did not receive such favor. Because the government saw her and the movement as a threat, she was eventually kidnapped and murdered along with two French nuns, Alice Domon and Léonie Duquet, who were in solidarity with the Mothers. Eventually the military leaders who ordered the death of these women were sentenced to life in prison for their crimes against the Mothers and other dissidents during the Dirty War.

We are blessed with the biblical story to help us observe and find application for our own conflicts and traumas. Art, music, print, and film have been employed to tell the story of the Mothers of the Plaza de Mayo. For the Mothers, documentaries and interviews can re-trigger the trauma for those who have experienced the loss of loved ones. We must remember this dynamic when we ask people to share their stories. Despite this fact, we have learned that storytelling in an instructive fashion helps to minimize re-traumatization. As new generations hear the stories, they gain access to wisdom, so that these things that never should have happened to anyone will never happen again.

The Mothers have continued their quest to keep looking for their children, eventually exposing new horrors including stories of torture and the revelation of mass graves. Heartbroken grandmothers uncovered the grim practice of stealing young children from detained women. The police and military stole the children who were then adopted by supporters of the regime. Detained pregnant women were even kept alive until they gave birth. After nursing their newborns for a few weeks, the women were dropped from helicopters into the ocean or the River Plate. The children were whisked away, to be raised by families viewed as politically acceptable. Over five hundred children of disappeared women were stolen in this way.[3] The Mothers, some now renamed Grandmothers of the Plaza de Mayo, have worked with human rights groups using DNA testing to reunite stolen children with their biological families.

Amid all their ongoing activism, the Mothers have had to attend to their surviving children and their marriages and handle the dynamics of simply working together with other women with mutual respect and care. The Mothers of the Plaza de Mayo continue today as seekers of justice, as Daughters of Rizpah, though divided. Some have focused on continuing the political dissidence of their children, and others have moved in the direction of government legislative reforms. Despite their differences, their courageous hearts command our attention and admiration. Truly the Mothers of the Plaza de Mayo are Daughters of Rizpah!

3. Goldman, "Children of the Dirty War."

12

CINDY SHEEHAN OF THE UNITED STATES

CINDY SHEEHAN IS A Daughter of Rizpah. She is best known for her August 6–31, 2005, encampment beginning in a ditch outside George W. Bush's ranch in Crawford, Texas. The president was spending those weeks on vacation at the ranch. Sheehan was there to protest the loss of her eldest son, Army Specialist Casey Austin Sheehan. He was killed during the Iraq War on April 4, 2004, only five days after arriving in Iraq. Like Rizpah, Cindy Sheehan camped out in a prolonged vigil, drawing global attention to what she believed was the immoral occupation of Iraq and the tragic cost in human lives, including that of her own precious son.

She felt a sense of shame that she had not tried earlier to prevent the war. She made up her mind to apply all her energy and time to stop the war, to prevent other mothers from losing their children. She was adamant about holding politicians accountable for their decisions to fund the war, a war she deemed immoral. She still believes her son did not die for freedom and democracy, rather he died to protect oil. "I believe that Casey and his buddies have been killed to line the pockets of already wealthy people and feed the insatiable war machine that has always devoured our young."[1]

---

1. Sheehan, *Peace Mom*, 117–18.

For Sheehan the core of her involvement was being a mother. She said: "I think it goes back to the motherhood thing. . . . We women carry the babies, we love them from the minute we know they're inside us. . . . My children have touched every part of me, even the inside of me. My kids were nourished inside of me for nine months and outside of me for up to eighteen months."[2] Mothering is where Sheehan's peace commitment came from, and not just for the protection of her children, but for all the children of the world. On that basis during the peace encampment, Sheehan tried to appeal to Barbara Bush, mother of the president. She wrote a letter that started, "Dear Barbara, On April 4, 2004, your oldest child George W. Bush killed my oldest child Casey Austin Sheehan."[3] Cindy received a letter from a mother in Iraq whose son was involved in the same battle in which Casey was killed. This soldier's mother expressed solidarity with Cindy saying, "I hope to be able to meet with you on the March for peace and love."[4] This Iraqi mother expressed solidarity with Sheehan, but Sheehan never got a reply from Barbara Bush.

Camp Casey was not the first peace action attempted by Sheehan. She originally tried to stop further violence by creating Gold Star Families for Peace in January 2005. Gold Star mothers are moms who have lost a child killed in a war while serving in the US military. Sheehan wanted to expand the Gold Star mission to include all family members affected by the death of a military service member. She got the idea at the Eyes Wide Open: The Human Cost of War conference sponsored by the American Friends Service Committee at the same time as the presidential inauguration for George W. Bush's second term. The exhibition included combat boots, one pair for each US military casualty during the recent wars in Afghanistan and Iraq.

It took some time for the horrible pain of her grief to grow into the passion to address the leaders who demanded the life of Casey. Sheehan found a sympathetic ear in a Michigan congressman. On

2. Sheehan, *Dear President Bush*, 14.

3. Sheehan, *Dear President Bush*, 77.

4. Sheehan, *Dear President Bush*, 106.

June 16, 2005, Cindy Sheehan testified before Congressman John Conyers regarding the Downing Street memo written by British foreign policy aide Matthew Rycroft. This memo proved that President Bush invaded Iraq on "thin" evidence of Saddam Hussein harboring weapons of mass destruction in conjunction with terrorist attacks on the United States in 2001. Sheehan thought that the revelation of the Downing Street memo and her testimony would rock the country and raise a hue and cry that would bring the war to an end. That did not happen.

Other documents that were important to Sheehan were the 9/11 Commission reports dispelling the idea that Saddam Hussein had anything to do with the 9/11 tragedy. The Senate Intelligence Report also dispelled the fact that Saddam had anything to do with 9/11, and the Weapons of Mass Destruction report proved that Saddam had no WMDs or even any hope of acquiring any for over a decade. Furthermore, the Downing Street memo indicated that the Bush administration was planning on invading Iraq, no matter what.[5]

What prompted Sheehan's call to action that resulted in the creation of Camp Casey? On August 3, 2005, George W. Bush was on the news, with the message that "the families of the fallen can rest assured that their loved ones died for a noble cause." Sheehan had heard George Bush say this at the very moment she was typing an email to about three hundred people mourning the loss of fourteen Marines who had been killed in Iraq on that very day. All of the Marines were from a unit in Ohio that had lost another six Marines just a few days prior. Prompted by these deaths and the president's comments, Cindy Sheehan decided to go to Dallas to speak at the Veterans for Peace convention and then drive as far as she could to camp at Bush's vacation address in Crawford, Texas.[6]

Rizpah in her grief needed to draw attention to the actions of the nation's top leader, King David. Enraged by grief, Sheehan wanted a personal audience with President Bush. At times she even refers to him as King Bush. The president had declared that all

5. Sheehan, *Peace Mom*, 159.
6. Sheehan, *Peace Mom*, 133–36.

soldiers who gave their lives in the Iraq invasion died for a "noble cause." Cindy, like many others protesting the war, wanted to know exactly the nature of that cause. The "why" question is crucial to addressing trauma. Rarely does an answer arrive, or if it does, it cannot satisfy the soul-shaking grief of traumatic injustice.

Instead of answers, sometimes the trauma intensifies. Imagine Rizpah, day after day chasing away the determined birds and dogs that were ready to steal the flesh of her children. Sheehan's trauma intensified too with threats and more cruel words hurled in her direction. There had been reports that the police had threatened to arrest all protesters on site on Thursday, August 11, 2005, when Secretary of Defense Donald Rumsfeld and Secretary of State Condoleezza Rice would be at the president's nearby ranch. However, no arrests in connection with the protest were made. President Bush did speak to reporters at his ranch, saying: "I sympathize with Mrs. Sheehan. She feels strongly about her position, and she has every right in the world to say what she believes. This is America. She has a right to her position, and I thought long and hard about her position. I've heard her position from others, which is: 'Get out of Iraq now.' And it would be a mistake for the security of this country and the ability to lay the foundations for peace in the long run if we were to do so."[7]

Instead, Sheehan became very upset that President Bush said that the United States had to complete the mission to honor the sacrifices of the ones who have fallen. For months she had been asking herself why her son Casey was killed and "why would I want one more person killed?" She turned the president's phrase around: "We have to honor the sacrifices of our loved ones by completing the mission of peace and justice. It is time. Bring our troops home *now*!"[8]

Cindy Sheehan quotes that President Bush defined a terrorist as someone who kills innocent men, women, and children. "Am I the only one who sees the irony and stunning hypocrisy in the statement? Who do the leaders of the free world think are being

7. Silverman, "President Bush."

8. Sheehan, *Dear President Bush*, 50.

killed in Iraq? A well trained and organized army? Terrorists? This is who is been killed in Iraq: Living breathing human beings identical to Americans. The same as other human beings anywhere on earth just trying to go on about their lives, trying to survive in a war-torn country that was never a threat to America or to our way of life."[9]

The initial protest camp moved from drainage ditches on public land to some land provided nearby by a sympathetic local resident named Fred Mattlage. He offered two acres of land for the camp to move from the ditch in Crawford. This became Camp Casey 2. His cousin Bubba Mattlage had deliberately run over crosses that have been set up to commemorate the lives of sons and daughters lost in the war. Fred was embarrassed and ashamed of what his cousin had done, so he offered space to the camp.[10] At times, more than one hundred people were camped on the site. In total, more than 1500 people visited the camp from all around the world.

Many people thought Sheehan was crazy and called her a nut case or a radical militant protester. She denies this. She sees herself as a mainstream American since the majority of Americans wanted the fighting in the Middle East to be over. However, she spoke about the labels that get changed when one speaks out: "One thing I have learned on my journey is that if you love our country but hate what our government is doing you are labeled 'un-American' and a 'nut case.' But if you let your son be killed in a useless war and are obediently silent about it then you are the 'mother of a hero.'"[11] The stress and strain of being away from home, constantly on the road for protests and television appearances cost Sheehan her marriage of twenty-eight years to Patrick Sheehan. She left her home and marriage in June 2005.

Like all Daughters of Rizpah, one's world is forever changed by the grief and loss that violence creates, even the "official" and "sanctioned" violence of war. Like Rizpah, the grieving mother

9. Sheehan, *Dear President Bush*, 108–9.

10. Sheehan, *Peace Mom*, 162.

11. Sheehan, *Peace Mom*, 106.

in the biblical text, Sheehan created a vigil and raised her voice. Cindy Sheehan simply sat down. "I did something so simple on August 6, 2005. Anyone can do what I did on that scorchingly hot August day. . . . I sat down."[12] Rizpah had some honor restored to her sons when King David came to her to properly bury them. Not so for Sheehan. The president never came out to Camp Casey to speak to the grieving mother Cindy Sheehan. If he had, she would have ended her encampment and headed home.

Camp Casey became the place where protesters could show support to end the occupation of Iraq by the US military. Before Sheehan's actions, there really was not much of an anti-war movement organized or evident. But Camp Casey was the spark that reignited the peace movement in the United States related to the invasion of Iraq. On September 24, 2005, more than 5,000 citizens protested in Washington, DC. For many it was their first ever protest or demonstration.[13] Sheehan can rightfully be credited with inspiring such new life into the anti-war movement.

The camp closed on August 31, 2005, but the efforts continued with the Bring Them Home Now tour. All leftover supplies from Camp Casey were moved to New Orleans for Hurricane Katrina relief. Cindy Sheehan continued to tour the United States until the peace rally in Washington, DC, where she set up Camp Casey, DC. Her message? No more wars for greed that kill generations. Over 500,000 peace activists showed up in Washington, DC, that September.

One of her supporters made her aware of a new term: "Matriot." A matriot is in contrast to a patriot. Matriots would do anything to stop killing as a way to solve problems. A matriot would never send her child or another mother's child to fight nonsense wars. According to Sheehan patriots hide behind the flag and recruit young people to die in order to fill their own pocketbooks. The women who flocked to Camp Casey spoke as advocates for true and lasting peace.[14]

12. Sheehan, *Peace Mom*, 240.
13. Sheehan, *Peace Mom*, 157.
14. Sheehan, *Dear President Bush*, 111–14.

Cindy Sheehan continues her protest to the present day via social media on Facebook and her own blog. With Rizpah-like persistence, she has been relentless in her analysis and passion to bring about peace around the world. Her motivation is to "retrieve our naive American souls from the soul-stealers who don't come in the dead of night, but steal our souls in broad daylight with no remorse."[15]

Sheehan is the author of three books: *Not One More Mother's Child*, *Dear President Bush*, and *Peace Mom*. She has protested the billions of dollars authorized for the wars in Iraq and Afghanistan. She left the Democratic Party, denouncing the "political expediency" of funding military operations in the region. She pronounced, in prophetic fashion, "You think giving him [Bush] more money is politically expedient, but it is a moral abomination, and every second the occupation of Iraq endures, you all have more blood on your hands."[16] Her current venue for protest is as executive producer and host at "Cindy Sheehan's Soapbox Radio Show." She can be found on Facebook as Cindy Sheehan. Cindy Sheehan is a Daughter of Rizpah!

---

15. Sheehan, *Peace Mom*, 237.
16. Quoted by Walsh, "'This Anti-Russia Campaign Is Horrible.'"

13

SUTHASINI SUTHAKARAN OF SRI LANKA

THE CLIMAX OF THE twenty-seven-year long civil war in the island nation of Sri Lanka came to a horrific definitive crescendo in the final battle in the Kilinochchi District, compressing in the end to the small northwest coastal area of Mullaitivu in May 2009. Suthasini Suthakaran, more commonly called Sutha, is a Tamil woman from Kilinochchi in northern Sri Lanka. Her family was among the civilians trapped in the Sri Lankan Army cordon. There was no way to escape the trauma of the last days of that war. In the time that followed, Sutha became a leader in the journey toward healing for many people and a prophetic voice about the needless suffering that so many endured.[1]

The war was a struggle by minority Tamils, mostly Hindus, seeking independence from the majority Sinhalese, mostly Buddhists. The Liberation Tigers of Tamil Eelam (LTTE or Tamil Tigers, more popularly) led the independence struggle. The Tigers were a very sophisticated liberation army even with some air and naval capabilities. They often used acts of terror and assassination.

1. The sources of this chapter are extensive author interviews in August 2017 with Sutha Suthakaran and with Jude Sutharshan, former principal of the Christian Theological Seminary in Jaffna, Sri Lanka, as well as visits to the Kilinochchi District and Mullaitivu and interviews with other war widows and Sutha's surviving family members.

The Sri Lankan Army was supported by a nationalist Buddhist ideology that heightened the ethnic and religious dimensions of the conflict. Around one hundred thousand people died in the conflict, with approximately forty thousand people killed in the final six months, mostly civilians. This was the context that swept up Sutha and her family.

As the Sri Lankan Army began its final offensive, tens of thousands of civilians were trapped in Mullaitivu with the Indian Ocean to the west and the army on the other three sides. Tamil Tiger fighters were hiding among the civilians, sometimes preventing the desperate and terrified civilians from fleeing to the other side. The army deliberately and repeatedly targeted hospitals, prompting the withdrawal of international aid organizations. Army artillery barrages often intentionally targeted mass gatherings of displaced civilians. Sutha was with her husband, who was not a fighter, and two daughters, ages two-and-a-half and ten. Sutha's husband was initially injured in the elbow with a shell fragment. With no medical treatment the wound festered. Sutha's sister was also injured while running and carrying her five-year-old child. A shell exploded, killing the child and maiming her sister's hand.

Four days before the war ended the Tamil civilians and fighters were jammed into a Mullaitivu beach area near the ocean. The heavy shelling continued, and Sutha's husband suffered a massive head injury. He pleaded with Sutha to take their daughters to find a trench for shelter. She left her husband on the beach, seeking a safe place for her children. When she was able to get them into the cover of a trench, Sutha went back to try to assist her husband. She never found him. She saw countless mangled bodies quickly bloating in the tropical heat and impossible to distinguish, the result of Sri Lankan Air Force carpet-bombing among the civilians.

After the war ended, Sutha and her children were sent to a displaced persons camp run by the military. The conditions of the camp were so deplorable that organizations such as the International Red Cross refused to participate. She tried desperately to find her husband. Some people called her saying they had him and demanded money to release him. Other women would sell whatever they had after receiving such calls, but nobody was ever reunited with a loved one through these heartless scams. Sutha decided not to pay such predators.

After a year in the camp she was allowed to return home. Her house had been destroyed. The whole village was in ruins. Seeing the devastation, Sutha lost all hope and contemplated suicide. She talked with her girls about how they would do it, perhaps mixing poison with tea. Instead she was found by someone working for a non-governmental organization who took her to a temporary shelter, a mere hut.

Pastors from nearby churches began working with the survivors. They organized inter-religious funerals for the dead. They used flowers to remember the dead. Such rituals helped Sutha begin to accept the reality of what had happened, though she continued to cry often, feeling she was breaking inside. She hated to think of herself as a "widow" because widows were scorned by the society. However, when she acknowledged she was a widow, a shift began as she started thinking about other widows, people who had been through similar traumatic events.

She signed up as a preschool teacher with a small salary and said to herself, "I can survive." She met other people and started to hear their stories. She began to get outside herself and her loss and see a larger community of people affected by the war.

Through the church, she was invited to go to Bangalore, India, to attend a center for peace and reconciliation studies. She learned how to work with women affected by war, women like herself. They explored the traditional cultural expectation for widows not to wear colorful saris, jewels, or decorate themselves. They discussed together whether such dictates needed to be followed. Sutha decided she could wear a flower in her hair or a colorful sari; she began to see herself as a person. She also learned to tell her story, and through the power of her own narrative came to understand the pain in her heart as a short-term sickness. There were also people who were willing to help; she did not need to be alone.

When Sutha came back from India, she immediately got to work. She organized a group of women, war widows like her. She didn't have any awareness of what she was going to do, but at least they could be together. Over thirty women gathered. They talked about the various issues they faced. They shared their stories of trauma and loss. They also helped each other with the challenges they faced, such as getting a new leg for a woman who had a very crude prosthetic. Eventually the group started their own credit union to help in paying school fees and providing small business start-up loans. All the loans could be paid back with no interest.

However, their biggest concern was the journey of healing. There was much social stigma attached to being a single woman, particularly a widow, so the women focused on personal empowerment supported by each other. Sutha was invited to attend a Tamil seminary, and through the seminary they were able to access stories and resources of other people with major social trauma history. They affirmed that every story needed to be heard, but this was counter-cultural in the context of the victorious government that was unwilling for the truth to be brought out. Though most of the women in Sutha's group were Hindu, they were all deeply moved and empowered by the story of Jesus with the Samaritan woman at the well. These Tamil widows connected with the Samaritan woman who was viewed as a non-person by her community. Contrary to the put-downs and discrimination toward widows in their own society, the Tamil widows were moved that Jesus knew this woman's story and invited her to deeper healing. This strengthened their commitment to their own quests for healing.

Sutha's advocacy began in some of the community meetings she attended. Military intelligence personnel would often show up at events and question Sutha about whether she was part of the LTTE. She would counter, "You are the people who killed my husband." The military intelligence people would respond that it wasn't the military but the LTTE who killed him. Like Rizpah, Sutha's words and actions spoke blunt truth to power.

As a part of reconciliation efforts the National Council of Churches sponsored a meeting in the Sri Lankan capital of Colombo. A Sri Lankan Army general participated in the Colombo event. He was a Christian and had been a major commander in the final offensive as well as second-in-command for civilian assistance and coordination following the war. Sutha was invited to the conference along with other Tamil women. When the general addressed the conference, he explained that he was in charge of all five rehabilitation camps following the war. He was proud about what he did. He told about taking care of orphaned LTTE children. "They called me father," he boasted. Then Sutha pushed him, "Were you there during the final battle?" The general answered, "Yes, I was there. I was in Jaffna in the north." She pressed further, "Are you a Christian?" "Yes," he replied. "How did you feel about all these things as a Christian?" The pride went out of this military commander. He put his head down and was silent for a while. Finally he mumbled, "It was horrible." The general was finally confronted by someone neither awed by him nor given to offering superficial compliments to someone in power. He had met Sutha, a Daughter of Rizpah! Interestingly, this general in the years following the war has become engaged in many activities to help the restoration of the Tamil community as part of reconciliation efforts. Sutha's advocacy was likely a key voice in bringing the full scope of the war's horrors to him, and like King David, this general joined in efforts of transformation.

Sutha continued her seminary studies, graduating just as this book went to press. She hopes to become a full-time minister, one of the first ordained women in her denomination. She plans to continue her work with traumatized women, especially among the widows. Sutha Suthakaran is a Daughter of Rizpah.

14

ROSETTE MANSOUR OF LEBANON

ROSETTE MANSOUR IS A Daughter of Rizpah! A citizen of Lebanon, Rosette, her unborn child, and her ten-month-old son, Marvin, were within moments of losing their lives at gunpoint from Syrian soldiers during the Lebanese Civil War. But over time, as a follower of Jesus, Rosette sensed Jesus nudging her toward forgiveness and love for her enemies. She now serves as senior partner relations officer for the Lebanese Society for Educational and Social Development in Beirut. Given the estimated population of Lebanon at 5.9 million in 2019, the 1.5 million Syrian refugees make Lebanon the country with the highest number of refugees per capita with one refugee for every four nationals. Rosette regularly visits with Syrian refugees, listening with her heart, and meeting needs however she can.

In her own words, Rosette writes,

> October 13, 1990, a day I will never forget—the last day of the civil war in Lebanon: I woke up at 7:15 a.m. at the sound of heavy bombs falling from every corner and from the planes above us; our house was so filled with smoke that I could barely see my son of ten months old. I grabbed him and ran to a "somehow" safer room. We were living in an area called Beit Mery—Al Qalaa, a

Christian area that was invaded first by the Syrian because it overlooks Baabda area where the presidential
palace is. The shelling was so fierce; we knew it was the
end. We decided that if we stayed at home, the Syrian
army would cross the valley and come and slaughter us,
but if we flee, we might have a slim chance to survive—or
die by a bomb which is an easier death than being slaughtered. So, we decided to leave the house and try to reach a
close by hotel where we can hide in their basement.

We drove for about five hundred meters on debris
and exploded bombs before we were stopped by the army.
As soon as we saw them we shouted, "WE ARE WITH
YOU! WE ARE WITH YOU!" but to our horror, they
were Syrian army coming to kill everybody on their way.
They asked us to step out of the car, put us on the wall
with our hands up, prepared their guns to shoot us. My
mind froze, everything was happening so quickly. I was
scared more than my mind can imagine. I was pregnant
with my daughter and carrying my ten-month-old son
up in the air. I couldn't imagine the situation. I had no
exit but to whisper a little prayer with eyes full of tears:
Lord, I can't see my family dying in front of me, please
let me die first. Then I heard a big explosion. I opened
my eyes thinking I'd be in heaven, but to my surprise, we
were still alive.

At that time, it happened that a Lebanese tank saw
the Syrians and threw a bomb on them. We were stuck
in the middle. The Syrian troops died. We were only five
meters away, but nothing hit us, not even the shrapnel
of the shells or its smoke. We ran to the car, drove to a
close-by house—we didn't know the people—and hid
there until 2:30 p.m. This is when they declared the end
of the civil war and the fall of our government.

That was a happy ending. God granted me the life
that I didn't even have faith to pray for. I came home
praising God and cleaning the house. I was so happy for
I saw death—that close—but God granted me life. But
the story didn't end here. The Syrians occupied our land
until 2005. They invaded homes, killing people—including children, kidnapping some and until now we don't
know where they are. . . . So, this was a terrifying chaotic

period. I had nightmares. I couldn't sleep. I was TERRI-FIED, and as a result, I couldn't bear seeing a Syrian or hearing their accent.

During that time, I was working at the [Arab Baptist Theological] Seminary, and we have Syrian students there. I knew I needed a miracle to forget because the fear was beyond my capacity to handle, so I prayed and fasted, and after five years I felt that I forgave and forgot—until the Syrian war started [in 2011] and they came [as refugees] to our country.

At that time, I knew what God wanted me to do, and I was afraid I couldn't act like the Good Samaritan. I can't visit, I can't see them face to face, so I told God I will be praying for them, and I honestly did.

The Syrian families were everywhere in Lebanon. In our tiny area of Mansourieh, we could locate more than four hundred families, so my son (who was ten months old and was about to be killed by the Syrians during the Civil War) and my daughter-in-law started visiting them and serving them, and every time we gather as a family for lunch on Sundays, all what they talk about are miracles that are happening among the Syrians. I still remember very well that Sunday afternoon. We were having coffee after lunch, and my son was sharing these two stories:

- Distribution of monthly food vouchers: We receive from MERATH[1] 120 food vouchers for distribution, but we have a list of 400 families, so we have more than 280 families on the waiting list. So my son was distributing the vouchers, and he has the last voucher that was about to expire in two days. He called the family that was supposed to take the voucher, but they returned back to Syria. So he called the first name on the waiting list; but this family was visiting their relatives in the Bekaa, and they weren't to return any time soon. So, my son called the second family—no reply, then the third—also no reply. So, he doesn't know why he skipped the fourth

1. Middle East Revive and Thrive, the relief arm of the Lebanese Society for Education and Social Development.

family and decided to visit the fifth one on the waiting list. A little boy of ten years old opened the door and told my son, "I know who you are, and we were waiting for you." The boy and his family didn't have anything to eat, when the boy went to bed not knowing what he will eat tomorrow, he saw Jesus in his dreams walking on water—this is a Muslim boy who has never heard the story of Jesus walking on water—when the boy asked him who are you, the reply was: "I'm Jesus. Don't worry. Tomorrow a man will visit you, and he'll bring you help. He will share with you about hope, love, and peace;" and He repeated these three times before the boy woke up.

- The story of the Syrian guy who came to Lebanon. At the beginning of the war, his dad was still in Syria. When the situation deteriorated around his area in Syria, he decided to flee in his Mercedes and all his money, $5,000. On the way, he was kidnapped by a fanatic party. They kidnapped him, took his car and his money. His son called my son, Marvin, asking him to pray so that they would release his father. Marvin prayed with no faith. How can they free his dad? Knowing the kidnapping party and how hard it is—a week later, the guy called Marvin saying they released his dad. Then he asked him to pray to return his car. So, again with little faith, my son prayed. Five days later, the guy called saying they returned the car in good condition—and that was the end of the conversation. Then one week later, the guy called saying: "I didn't ask you to pray for them to return the money, but I prayed in the name of Marvin's God, if you are a living God and if you hear prayers let them return the money, and they did. Because I know your God answers prayers."

When I heard these two stories, I couldn't resist. I can't see God at work, doing miracles without me being involved. This is when I started visiting, caring, and holding Discovery Bible Study for Syrian women every week. But every morning when I wake up, the verse "love your enemy" echoes in my head, and I would argue with God:

"Isn't it enough I give them my time? Isn't it enough I put
my energy there?" . . . But the verse kept echoing in my
head. Until one morning, I woke up, and the verse didn't
echo in my head—this is when I realized that by serving
others, God healed me from being self-centered—caught
in my own trauma—and He taught me the true meaning
of the verse "love your enemies."[2]

Rosette's story humbles us. In the cycle of trauma, we admire
Rosette for her courage to resist becoming stuck in hatred and fear.
At first, Rosette admits she was jealous of the amazing miracles
she was seeing in her son's ministry. She shared that Marvin has a
passion for the Syrian people because he knows his own story of
how he nearly lost his life as a baby. So through her son, Rosette
began to explore how she could move out and beyond her trauma.

Rosette was guided by her faith and desire to serve God, to
see the "enemy" as a human being in need of help. This sparked
her compassion, but that was not enough. Her compassion had
a shadow side: She discovered her acts of compassion were still
tainted by a victim identity within herself. The power of the
trauma was still lurking in the background of her soul. She named
this as "self-centered" and "trauma-focused." This is the place God
longed to heal in her. Agape love is unconditional love that seeks
no response and expects nothing in return. It is a selfless, God-
centered love, flowing from God through us to others. This is the
love that healed Rosette and in turn gave her peace to serve in true
forgiveness.

Daughters of Rizpah like Rosette know that there is no guarantee that one's actions will be appreciated or well received. Rizpah
grieved for months in public and many of those days of mourning
were spent without reward. But Daughters of Rizpah don't settle!
There is perseverance, a long-suffering work that takes the victim
of trauma through a process of inner transformation and a hope
that God will act. Rosette was rewarded with inner peace and the
transformation of her enemies into allies and friends.

2. From an unpublished personally written paper Rosette Mansour gave
to the authors during an extensive interview in March 2019. Used with
permission.

Daughters of Rizpah also struggle with the desire to "forgive and forget." It seems to be humanly impossible to forget the terrors of trauma. But Rosette learned to remember the trauma in a different way, to carry it differently so she could relate to her former enemy. Sharon's definition of forgiveness embraces this idea: "Forgiveness is being willing to carry the hurt that others have caused us, for the sake of the relationship. Even if someone chooses not to acknowledge the relationship verbally or tangibly, the emotional relationship remains." Hurts do wound and burden us, but we can choose to hold them in our hands, look at them, and name them, then turn them over to the One who carries them with us and for us. Instead of forgetting, our memories are transfigured.

Jesus promises us in Matt 11:28–30 that we can come to him and rest. "Come to me, all you that are weary and are carrying heavy burdens, and I will give you rest. Take my yoke upon you, and learn from me; for I am gentle and humble in heart, and you will find rest for your souls. For my yoke is easy, and my burden is light." The Greek word for "weary" or "labor" is *kopaio* and indicates a kind of labor that is exhausting and wearying to the soul. It is the kind of labor that comes from a hardship assignment in military terms, a difficult job that goes on long beyond what seems humanly possible. That sounds like the burden of trauma!

In verse 29, Jesus said, "Take my yoke upon you." The word "take" is the word *airo,* meaning to deliberately lift or to deliberately take up. Our responsibility seems to be that we must intentionally ask Jesus to "yoke" with us, to combine the strength we need to carry the load of trauma that is too difficult to carry alone. The promise is that God pulls with us and is, in fact, the stronger one pulling the load. Here Jesus also promises the presence of one who will not be separated from us in the task and the journey.

Rosette lives daily in this spirituality, drawing her inspiration and strength from Jesus. The result is this woman so traumatized by her near-execution experience yet she is serving people of the same background as her would-be executioners in their time of need. Rosette Mansour is a Daughter of Rizpah!

15

LEYMAH GBOWEE OF LIBERIA

Pray the Devil Back to Hell[1] is a documentary film about the praying women of Liberia who are true Daughters of Rizpah. This documentary tells the story of the praying women who brought an end to one of the most vicious wars in recent history. Liberian President Charles Taylor had said he could pray the devil out of hell. A courageous band of Liberian women said they would pray the devil back to hell, and they did!

In the early 2000s, Liberia was being destroyed by a long and brutal civil war. Rizpah, a biblical woman tormented by grief and injustice, took nonviolent action and committed civil disobedience, protecting the flesh and bones of her dead sons. In Liberia, the Muslim and Christian women did the same. They mobilized in grief and cried out about the horrific injustice plaguing Liberia. They came together in a prayer movement that had a powerful outcome of lasting peace in Liberia.

Civil war broke out in Liberia in 1989, led by Charles Taylor and his child soldiers, some as young as nine years old. The atrocities of violence and war committed during that civil war were terrifying and left more than one hundred thousand dead and countless others maimed for life. The rape of women by soldiers was rampant,

---

1. *Pray the Devil Back to Hell.* Chapter quotes come from this documentary.

and thousands of people were displaced by the war. Sam Doe, the earlier president who came to power in a violent coup, was killed; and then Taylor was elected president in 1997. However, Taylor's election brought no peace. Rebel movements quickly surfaced, and the renewed brutality and violence spun out of control.

Then a Daughter of Rizpah came onto the scene: Leymah Gbowee. She was intimate with the horrors of war, particularly as a mother. She once fled her village while it was under attack at a time when she was five months pregnant and had a three-year-old son and two-year-old daughter. Having no food as they fled, Gbowee experienced the maternal anguish of having nothing to give her hungry children. Later, Gbowee became a social worker with an emphasis on trauma counseling. In that capacity she often worked with former child soldiers, seeing up close the damage done to their young lives by the horrific violence in which they had participated.

Gbowee believed in the power of prayer, and in 2002 she organized women in her church to pray for peace. This time, however, they prayed with a difference. Instead of praying inside the church, they gathered at the fish market alongside the main thoroughfare of Monrovia. They caught the attention of Muslim women who also wanted to pray. Some debate occurred: Could women of different faiths pray together? They decided that the "bullet does not discriminate" in robbing the lives of their children and families, so they began to pray together for peace, forming the Women In Peacebuilding Network.

Armed with prayer and wearing distinctive white T-shirts, the women organized in displaced persons camps all across Liberia. The women sang and prayed. They also initiated sex strikes, refusing to have sexual intercourse with their husbands and demanding that the men lay down their weapons and organize for peace efforts. Using radio to announce their actions the women took to the streets and organized public prayer vigils, drawing upon the example of Queen Esther of Persia in the Bible. Esther was a courageous woman who mobilized her community inside and outside her palace to pray. She successfully confronted King

Ahasuerus[2] about a genocide planned for the Jews, Esther's ethnic and religious community.

On his way from his mansion to the Presidential Office Building, President Charles Taylor had to pass by as many as twenty-five hundred women praying and holding up signs at the fish market. At first he ignored the women of Liberia gathered there—to his peril, because these Daughters of Rizpah were not to be denied! The women marched on the Presidential Office Building demanding that Taylor participate in peace talks. They also traveled to neighboring countries to meet insurgent leaders. The women appealed to these warlords, speaking as the mothers of Liberia, demanding that the rebels join the talks.

Eventually, spurred by the insistent and persistent women, peace talks were held in Accra, Ghana. Initially progress was slow to nonexistent. Then, Gbowee and many of the other women went to Accra and maintained a vigil outside the hotel where the talks were being held. During the talks, Taylor was indicted for war crimes related to Sierra Leone, and he fled to Nigeria for safety. Immediately it seemed all hell broke loose back in Liberia as the rebels launched a new ferocious assault on Monrovia. For six weeks the women in Ghana went back and forth between the delegations in Ghana demanding peace. Every day they were receiving desperate messages from their families and the other praying women back home that the violence was out of control.

A turning point took place on July 21, 2003, when the US embassy in Monrovia was hit by rockets that fell among the hundreds of displaced people camping inside the compound. This atrocity fueled fresh anger in Leymah Gbowee, whose frustration was building over the inaction at the peace conference. So she proclaimed: "Today is the showdown." Gbowee led the women into the hotel where the talks were being held and had them sit at the door of the conference hall with their arms looped together. The women blocked the delegates from coming in or going out. Gbowee said, "We're going to keep them in that room without water, without

2. The king is called Xerxes in some translations, such as the New International Version.

food, so they at least feel what the ordinary people in Liberia are feeling at this particular point in time." As the women took their places someone announced over the hotel loudspeaker: "Oh, my God, the peace hall has been seized by General Leymah and her troops!" The Ghanaian police came to arrest Gbowee on charges of disrupting justice. That charge was the final insult to Gbowee, deeming the warlords inside as the ones who were shredding justice for her country. So in front of the police Gbowee stood and began to strip off her clothes. In West Africa it is a curse to see the naked body of one's mother, or any older woman for that matter. Gbowee's action prompted a quick and desperate response by the police. The police backed down and soon were assisting the women in their blockade by pointing out windows where delegates were trying to climb out so the women could block those exits.

General Abdulsalami Abubakar, the lead mediator from Nigeria, sided with the women and their demands that the parties to the peace talks get serious about their task. He got the Liberian government representatives and the rebel leaders to accept the women's demands and to stop insulting the praying women on their way into the conference hall. A peace agreement was reached within the two-week deadline forced by the women.

Following the terms of the peace accord a transitional government was formed. United Nations peacekeeping troops were brought in to help stabilize the country. The women under Gbowee's leadership continued to be active, overseeing amnesty and weapons surrender programs throughout Liberia. In November 2005 Ellen Johnson Sirleaf was elected president, and in her inaugural address in January 2006 the first woman president elected in Africa gave a profound expression of thanks to the praying women who put their bodies on the line to end the war. In 2011 Leymah Gbowee and Ellen Johnson Sirleaf were awarded the Nobel Peace Prize.

These courageous women put a full stop to ruling warlords. Through their prayers, persistence, and protests, peace was at long last established in their country. Leymah Gbowee and all the praying Christian and Muslim women of Liberia are Daughters of Rizpah!

16

MOTHERS OF SREBRENICA
FROM BOSNIA AND HERZEGOVINA

SREBRENICA WAS THE SITE of the worst massacre in Europe since World War II. As Yugoslavia broke up into different independent countries, some of the break-up conflicts exploded into wars including the war in Bosnia and Herzegovina. The conflict in Bosnia, as it is more often called, pitted ethnic Serbs (mostly Orthodox), ethnic Croats (mostly Catholic), and Muslims (sometimes called Bosniaks) against one another. Though all sides committed atrocities, the Serbian militias[1] were notorious for their brutality and human rights violations, some of which ended up with trials and convictions after the war in the International Criminal Court in The Hague.

Srebrenica is a town nestled in the beautiful wooded mountains of Bosnia. It had been an ethnically mixed town. On July 11, 1995, Serbian militiamen seized control of the area. They quickly rounded up all the males they could find and massacred them. More than eight thousand men and boys and even toddlers were killed. Their bodies were dumped in mass graves. The

---

1. Many media reports use the terms "Serb militia" and "Croat militia," though we will use the adjective form of the ethnic terms.

Muslim women were driven out, leaving Srebrenica as an "ethnically cleansed" community.

Hatidža Mehmedović was one of those exiled women. Before the Serbian offensive she had lived with her husband Abdullah and two sons Azmir, twenty-one years old, and Almir, eighteen years old, in the village of Vidikovac near Srebrenica. As the Serbian militias pushed out the Croatian and Bosniak militias out of the area, tens of thousands of Muslim civilians fled for refuge to Srebrenica where United Nations Peacekeepers from The Netherlands had created a supposed safe zone. However, when the Bosnian Serbian militia under the command of General Ratko Miladić swept into Srebrenica, the Dutch battalion simply stood aside, leaving the civilians at the mercy of Miladić and his men. Mehmedović recalled her last moments with her husband and sons as the women were evacuated by bus: "We were standing there and my young one, Lalo—that's what we called him, although his name was Almir—was saying, 'Go on, mother, go, leave, already' as he was pulling me closer and closer, and would not let me go. . . . We thought we'd see each other in two, three days. We did not know they'd kill them all."[2]

At first, the women were relocated near Tuzla, then later Mehmedović moved near Sarajevo. In 2002 she decided to return to her pre-war home in Vidikovac. That same year she organized the Mothers of Srebrenica and became its first president. The group was established to advocate for justice for the victims and to collect and distribute aid to the surviving families. She spoke before many groups throughout Europe. At a Srebrenica memorial event in the United Kingdom Mehmedović spoke in a way that echoes what Rizpah might have said: "I am a woman who lives in Srebrenica alone. I am a woman that once had a husband. I am a mother that gave birth to two sons. But I have no one anymore. I go to bed alone and I wake up alone. I gave birth to children who played, went to school, who laughed, yet all I had to bury were just two bones."[3]

In their advocacy role, the Mothers of Srebrenica tried to bring a case against the United Nations, but the International

2. Surk, "Hatidža Mehmedović."
3. Remembering Srebrenica, "Remembering Srebrenica Mourns."

Criminal Court in The Hague determined that the UN had absolute immunity and could not be held liable. However, the Dutch government granted a measure of compensation to the survivors in recognition of the failure of the Dutch troops to maintain their safe zone. Later, when Ratko Miladić was tried for his war crimes, Mehmedović witnessed him being sentenced to life in prison. Though she was glad he was convicted she spoke about the many other war crimes committed where the perpetrators still had not been held to account.

Mehmedović occupied her old home in part to show the perpetrators that they had not succeeded. Though she worked to hold war criminals responsible for their murders, she also was determined to lift up and work toward a diverse and reconciled Bosnia. She opposed growing nationalism and sectarianism. She was one of the first of the displaced Muslims to return home, as she was deeply committed to the vision of Bosniaks and Bosnian Serbs living together in peace. She helped her elderly Serbian neighbor with his shopping and chores. She stressed that she didn't blame Serbs as a people for what happened or hold any sense of collective guilt against them. This vision later took shape in the memorial established to remember the victims of the massacre.

A large memorial complex has been created in Srebrenica. Just inside the entrance is a huge circle of low, sloped, massive blocks of polished granite. Into the granite were carved the 8,372 names of the men and boys massacred there as well as the names of some women who were raped and then murdered. Each person's name is given as well as their age, ranging from infants to the elderly. On the eleventh of every month the Mothers of Srebrenica gather to commemorate the loss of their loved ones. They keep vigil as Rizpah did, but they have also spoken out through the stones in the memorial.

Near the circle of names is another granite stone, short and wide with the calligraphy script in Arabic used by Muslims for quotes from the Qur'an. The quote selected—stunning given the ongoing context of division in Bosnia and specifically Srebrenica—is this: "It may be that Allah will grant love and friendship between you and those whom you now hold as enemies" (Surah 60:7).[4] It is the victims who lift up the hope for reconciliation even when there is no indication of interest by the perpetrators of the crime or the community from which they came.

As international workers have been unearthing the mass graves, they have gone through DNA testing to identify the remains of those killed. As some of the remains are identified, they are reburied in separate graves with marked stones. Among those identified were the husband and sons of Hatidža Mehmedović, just a few bones, even as Rizpah ended up with just the bones of her loved ones.

Alongside this newer graveyard with identified remains is another granite block, narrow and high. The Mothers of Srebrenica had this prayer chiseled into the stone: "In the name of God the Most Merciful and Most Compassionate, we pray to Almighty God, may grievance become hope, may revenge become justice, and may mothers's tears become prayers that Srebrenica never happen again to no one, nowhere."[5] To no one, nowhere—not just to their own people, but to all people, even to those among the ethnic group that massacred their loved ones!

The Mothers of Srebrenica did not turn their grief into a desire for their enemies to die. They didn't perpetuate the cycles of violence, but rather prayed for an end to such ongoing retribution, hatred, and trauma. They wished their trauma on nobody else.

Hatidža Mehmedović died in 2018 at the age of sixty-five. Even as her health was failing she labored to provide support for refugees fleeing from the war in Syria to Europe. Her witness for justice and reconciliation is carried on by the other Mothers of Srebrenica. Hatidža Mehmedović and all the Mothers of Srebrenica are Daughters of Rizpah![6]

4. 'Ali, *Meaning of the Holy Qur'an*, 1454.

5. Rough translation on site by Fyodor Raychynets during a personal visit by Dan Buttry in March 2007.

6. Sources: Personal visit by Dan Buttry to Srebrenica and interviews with friends in Bosnia, International Crimes Database (www.internationalcrimes-database.org), and Remembering Srebrenica (www.srebrenica.org.uk).

EPILOGUE

Hope with Eyes Wide Open

OUR FRIEND JAN KRIST is a prolific and profound singer/song-writer. In one of our favorite songs she questions:

> What makes the abused refuse to back down?
> What makes the broken stand their ground?
> What makes the heart start to believe?
> What is the gift that faith receives?
> What is the soul of the mystery?
> And what breaks the hold of brutality?[1]

As we look at Rizpah and ponder the stories of the Daughters of Rizpah, these questions ring out. What made them act in such a bold way in the face of brutal violence? Why did they stand out as transformative when so many others either disappeared in their trauma or took revenge, descending into a destructive vortex of violence? How did they break the "hold of brutality" over them and within them?

Jan's answer is:

> Hope—with its eyes wide open
> Hope—with its will unbroken
> Hope!

Hope? There is anger. There is sorrow. There is desperation. But what rises up through these powerful emotions is an even

1. Krist, "Hope."

105

more powerful force, namely hope. Rizpah's hope is not a flimsy, wishful hope. She doesn't moan wishing the nightmare would go away. Rizpah and her daughters have a hope that may begin with an oath, "Damn it, this horror will not be the last word!" "Eyes wide open . . . will unbroken." This hope erupts strong and insistent, determined, and is not to be denied.

The verses of Jan's song plunge into the context that grinds people down, the context that causes some to shrink away and others to wrap themselves in a shield of cynicism:

> Let's talk about fear,
> Being afraid and the toll that it takes on us every day;
> Pain, grief, and doubt
> And the way that it pulls us inside out,
> You think that nothing is gonna change,
> Just leaves you a prisoner to the pain.
>
> And let's talk about
> What can become of the faith that we give
> And the things that are done,
> And faith in something bigger than us
> More true than the people who vie for our trust?
> 'Cause trust can be abused; truth can be betrayed,
> So how's anything gonna change?

This is the context of so many people around the world, dynamics that leave us feeling powerless and in despair. Nothing is going to change. Trust is shattered. Truth is proudly mocked by liars with power. What does it take to buck this tide and bring transformative change?

Jan's last chorus adds a line:

> It's you and me and
> Hope—with its eyes wide open
> Hope—with its will unbroken
> Hope!

Hope involves a choice, something we choose to lean into. Hope bubbles up from a well that is deeper than our pain, our anger, our fear, or our confusion. If there is a community of hope, then so much the better. Rizpah acted alone in the ancient story, but many of the Daughters of Rizpah found community to support their hope. The Mothers of Srebrenica, the Naga Mothers, COMADRES, and the Mothers of the Plaza de Mayo found their hope bolstered by their deeply committed relationships with one another. Sutha found solidarity in hope with other widows like her. Rosette found support from her son.

How can hope emerge when one has lost the most precious people in one's life? Sometimes the transformation comes from moving beyond one's own awful losses toward others who could face the same loss. Cindy Sheehan's hope was born in her desire to protect other mothers so they would not experience the overwhelming loss she had suffered. The Mothers of Srebrenica prayed their hope that "Srebrenica never happen again to no one, nowhere."

Sometimes the hope is vague and unfocused, but there is just enough light to take the next step. So Leymah Gbowee and the women of Liberia began with a simple vigil at the fish market where the president would pass by. When they placed themselves out in the public and with the support of one another, their hope crystalized into one action leading to the next until they forced the peace agreement crafted to end the war in Liberia.

Igniting hope may be the most radical gift a person can give to a struggle for justice or peace. Hope for people in a repressive or violent situation may seem comatose, ready for the last rites. But then someone arises, a Rizpah or a Daughter of Rizpah. She may be full of sorrow. She may be full of rage. She may feel shattered and shredded. Yet she feels something deep within, that small flame of hope. Others are too defeated to notice but she rises up. She speaks out. She risks everything. Then suddenly or gradually the light of hope shines brighter, fanned to flame in her bold action. When such hope ignites, it can unleash a life-giving, violence-halting, transformative wildfire.

In the Trauma Healing Journey the narrative of "good versus evil" takes on a new title—the story of "us." The new story is one that both the victim and offender can authentically claim as "our story." Our hope is that the stories of Rizpah and her daughters will ignite flames of hope within hearts shattered by the traumas of violence. Our prayer is that the new stories will overtake the narrative of endless cycles of violence. May Rizpah's daughters, and even her sons, lead us into a future where these hopes are fulfilled.

APPENDIX A

Merab or Michal?

THERE IS A QUESTION about who the mother of the five slaugh-tered boys really is. Some ancient texts and most contemporary translations identify the mother as Merab, but other ancient Greek and Hebrew texts and some translations in English and other languages name her as Michal.[1] Does it matter? In the arc of the narrative in our text, this mother is a victim who fades from the story whatever her name might be. So for this book we stuck with the majority opinion.

However, for accuracy and intrigue we will look at the alter-native, for Merab and Michal are two separate people with very different story lines apart from the particular narrative in 2 Sam 21. Merab is a relatively unremarkable character in the Davidic texts. First Samuel 18:17–19 tells of Saul actually offering his oldest daughter, Merab, to David in marriage, but at the last moment Saul changed his mind and married her off to Adriel of Meholah, a rela-tional identity affirmed in our text in 2 Sam 21:8. None of the texts mention any emotional connections between David and Merab.

Michal, however, is a very significant figure in the David sto-ries. If Michal is the mother of the five slaughtered sons, then a huge subplot opens up that is very interesting and intriguing but not germane to the main thread of the trauma and transformation story we are concerned with in this book.

1. For example in English see the King James Version, the American Stan-dard Version, and the Modern English Version.

Michal was Saul's daughter. As David was growing in his military success in the service to Saul, Saul began to cycle through fits of jealous anger that showed signs of mental illness. After Saul had broken the engagement of Merab to David he learned that his younger daughter Michal was in love with David. He plotted to marry her to David "so that she may be a snare to him" (1 Sam 18:20–21). He asked David for the bride-price of the foreskins of a hundred Philistines, hoping that David would be killed in such an overwhelming undertaking. David not only succeeded in the task, but he exceeded Saul's bride-price by bringing back two hundred Philistine foreskins. (Again, these ancient tales are not for the faint of heart!) So Saul went ahead with the marriage of Michal and David. The text concludes this particular story with a note about Michal's love and Saul's fear of David (1 Sam 18:28–29). When Saul's rages against David intensified to the point where David needed to flee, Michal urged him to escape. She helped David slip out of a window ahead of Saul's soldiers who had been sent to seize him. Then Michal cooked up a ruse putting an idol with a false wig of goat's hair in David's bed, telling the arresting soldiers that David was ill. After some back and forth the soldiers brought the supposed sickbed to Saul where the ruse was exposed. Saul was furious with Michal, and Michal said David threatened to kill her if she didn't aid his escape. All this activity bought David the time he needed to make his escape. (See the story particularly in 1 Sam 19:11–17.)

While David was on the run he married two other women, Abigail and Ahinoam. Saul meanwhile voided the marriage of David to Michal in some way, perhaps even by royal fiat, and gave Michal to Paltiel, only identified as the son of Laish from Gallim (2 Sam 25:44). No note is made of the feelings of any of those involved, but the new marriage created a new reality that would have significant import later.

The relationship between David and Michal takes a further twist following the death of Saul and the resultant civil war between the House of David and the House of Saul. Abner, the commander of the forces from Saul's side, negotiated an end to the fighting. As part of the deal David insisted that his first wife,

Michal, be restored to him. Saul's son Ishbaal[2] took Michal away from her current husband Paltiel. It is interesting that after all the mention of Michal's love in the earlier stories there is no mention of her emotions at all in this account. Rather the emotions noted are the intense grief of Paltiel who followed Abner as he carried Michal off to David. Abner ordered Paltiel to go back, and he did, a pathetic, broken footnote in the saga of the struggle for the throne of Israel (see 2 Sam 3:13–16).

Once David becomes king it is clear that the relationship between Michal and David has changed dramatically from the first episodes of their story. In 2 Sam 6 the civil war is over and David brings the Ark of the Covenant up to Jerusalem with great celebration and a magnificent procession. In his jubilation David dances in front of the ark, clad only in a linen ephod, a priestly apron. In verse 16 Michal watches David from a window and "despised him in her heart." Later when David returns home Michal confronts him about "uncovering himself today before the eyes of his servants' maids," comparing him to a "vulgar fellow" (v. 20). David harshly rebukes her saying God chose him over the House of Saul to be the ruler of Israel and that he would become even more undignified celebrating God. The slave girls Michal mentioned would hold David in honor, at least according to David.

The conclusion to the story in 2 Sam 6:23 is stark and poignant: "And Michal the daughter of Saul had no child to the day of her death." Does that mean that Michal never had any children? Possibly. However, if Michal is the mother in the 2 Sam 21 story, then there is added sorrow and horror to the tale and a complex relational twist. The sons would then likely have been Michal's sons from the grieving Paltiel, and Saul's grandsons. The text would be highlighting David's vengeance on a broken relationship that left Michal as a shattered old woman with nobody to care for her.[3]

---

2. Some translations, such as the New International Version, call this son of Saul Ish-Bosheth.

3. Cephas T. A. Tushima believes that Michal is the mother of the five slain sons. He lays out in great detail the twisted nature of David's actions against her and her sons (*Fate of Saul's Progeny*, 205–23).

APPENDIX B

Training Toolbox

Since 2003 we have been engaged in leading conflict transformation training in over forty-five countries around the world. The Rizpah story has been one of the most profound sections in our training design. The way in which we have used the story has evolved. Early on, the focus was on Rizpah finding her voice to speak out from the margins. Then we focused on her action as a nonviolent transforming initiative similar to the story about Burma/Myanmar in the Introduction. Now we use the story as the centerpiece for the topic of trauma as seen in the bulk of this book. For those interested in doing participatory experiential education as a part of peace building work or trauma healing, this appendix will give directions on using the Rizpah story as a tool in the training toolbox. (A wider selection of tools including those discussed in this appendix can be found at www.globalpeacewarriors.org/resources/toolbox. Most tools include photos showing what the tool looks like in action.)

We begin with various activities to set the stage for the trauma discussion. Sometimes we begin with group juggling (see below). For a group of twenty to thirty people that has already established significant safety in the group, we form small groups of two or three people and give the instruction to draw a picture of a trauma experience that they don't mind sharing with others. After drawing and sharing in the small group, participants are asked to come up with a generalized list of what they did or what others did that helped them deal positively with the trauma. We then harvest a list, recorded on newsprint at the front of the room, from the entire group.

Next we divide into working groups of five to eight people to plunge into the Bible study of 2 Sam 21, acknowledging that this is a difficult story. We pass out a worksheet with the following questions to be answered for each of the three traumatized people or groups, namely Merab, the Gibeonites, and Rizpah:

1) What did each person or group do in response to their trauma experience? What feelings do you imagine must have been a part of each response (perhaps even complex and contradictory feelings)?

2) What was the result of their response to trauma?

3) Was there any response of God that followed what they did in response to trauma? What might that indicate?

4) Give contemporary examples of these responses to trauma that you may have experienced or witnessed, if time allows.

We don't give any more priming about the study than this, believing that participants will get more out of the entire session if they personally grapple with the text and raise questions for themselves out of what they encounter.

After participants study the story we invite a participant to volunteer to be interviewed playing the character Merab or Michal. (We check out in advance which name is used in the most common translation where we are holding the training.) We sometimes set the interview up like a local television news broadcast trying to find out what happened in the recent incident. Male or female participants can be welcome in any of the interviews; some of our best interviews have been from people playing cross-gender roles. The role-play interview elicits many feelings of loss, anger, grief, confusion, etc. After the interview we introduce a printed handout and explore the theory of the Victim/Survivor Cycle, referencing dimensions of both the biblical story and what might have been expressed in the interview.

Then we interview Mr. or Ms. Gibeon, someone role-playing a member of the ethnic group that had earlier experienced genocide and then conspired with King David to execute seven of Saul's male descendants. We use the same format that was used in the first interview, such as an imaginary TV news show. We follow up the Mr. or Ms. Gibeon interview with the Aggressor/Offender Cycle handout and explanation of the cycle, again referencing the Bible story and what was expressed in the interview.

Usually after a break we dramatize the Rizpah story from beginning to end. A facilitator should be the narrator, sometimes also slipping in and out of David's role. We utilize Mr. or Ms. Gibeon from the interview in the skit to work with David in assembling the sons of Saul for execution, seven participants grabbed and placed in seven chairs set across the front. We act out David praying to God, discussing plans with Mr./Ms. Gibeon, seizing the sons, and slaying them. David and Mr./Ms. Gibeon can then shake hands and return to their places.

Then Rizpah enters, perhaps from outside the room or coming from the participant circle. A female facilitator could play Rizpah, or a facilitator could ask a female participant in advance to participate, briefing them on the role they should play. Rizpah should vocalize her grief dramatically, with wails, perhaps touching her slain sons. She should bring a scarf or shawl to vigil upon and to use to shoo away imaginary birds and dogs. The drama grows in intensity as the narrator lists out the months: April, May, June—what is happening to the bodies? They disintegrate. So the facilitator can use markers, sticks, or cut out paper as bones, inviting the "dead" to return to their seats and replace themselves with the "bones." The narrator continues the monthly count: June, July, August. What do people think about Rizpah? Perhaps she is crazy, maybe her neighbors are urging her to come home and be with Merab. But she remains—August, September, October—until David in his palace hears about what Rizpah is doing.

David then goes to Jabesh-gilead to gather the bones of Saul, Jonathan, and the others killed at Mt. Gilboa, (bones that have earlier been deposited at the place in the room to be that distant village.) Then with those bones David comes and encounters Rizpah with humility, maybe even kneeling before Rizpah. Together they gather the symbolic bones of the seven, and take them to a far place in the room representing the ancestral tomb. The narrator then concludes, "Then God healed the land!"

We follow up the Rizpah drama with a detailed exploration of the Trauma Healing Journey handout, including many references to steps taken by Rizpah and David in the story that illustrate that process. Constructing a new narrative is seen in the fact that the story in the Bible is a complex one rather than a simple "good versus evil" story such as appears in the cycles of violence. If there is time and interest in the group we will also encourage further discussions about David's experience with trauma and transformation as well as the question of where God is and isn't in the story.

To close the session we might invite participants to name and perhaps tell stories about contemporary Rizpahs. We might have a memorialization exercise, lighting candles and naming names of those to be remembered. In some workshop designs we then move into the topic of reconciliation processes.

Notes for Group Juggling

Group juggling is a useful tool for learning names and team building in groups of twelve to twenty people. Supplies include three or four small balls (tennis ball size, but tennis balls can be too bouncy). It adds to the fun to have different kinds of balls or even a small item that can be thrown, such as a small stuffed animal. All the balls should be fairly soft.

Have the group form a circle. With one ball, make a practice run of the exercise to establish a pattern that will be repeated always the same way. Instruct the participants to call out the name of the person they will throw the ball to and make eye contact with them before throwing the ball. To begin, the facilitator will throw the ball to one person, who in turn will throw the ball to a different person. Each participant throws the ball to the same person every time, remembering to first say their name and make sure the recipient is ready to catch the ball. Keep tossing the ball around the circle to people who have not yet received the ball until everyone has received the ball once. The last person to receive the ball will then throw it to the person who started the cycle.

After the first practice run, continue the pattern, throwing the ball to the same person and speeding up the process. After it seems the group has the idea and is following the pattern well, introduce a second and then third or even fourth ball.

After a few minutes as people are having fun and improving you can stop the game to debrief. Debriefing questions can cover topics such as what it took to successfully do the task, what enabled the group to improve, etc.

Trauma Awareness Variation

This is an emotionally low-risk variation of group juggling that can be used to simulate trauma when group participants may not know each other very well. The variation works best with fifteen to twenty-five participants. The facilitator will not be a participant in the group juggling but will stay outside the circle, providing instructions to get the game started. Alternatively, if there is a co-facilitating team, one person can lead the group juggling, and the other facilitator can carry out the trauma simulation part of the activity.

Begin the group juggling activity as described above. Instruct the group to keep the process going. After the group is well into the game, the facilitator (or co-facilitator) gently pulls one of the participants out of the circle, perhaps saying, "Come with me." The person is removed from the room or to a distant edge of the room. Let the group deal with the resulting confusion and try to find a new pattern. Then remove a second person, then later a third person.

When you stop the game bring those pulled out back into the circle. Use open-ended elicitive questions to debrief about initial feelings, how awareness about the loss of a person developed, how the group members felt about the loss, how leadership emerged to develop new patterns, and what successive losses felt like. After debriefing members in the circle, ask those who had been removed what some of their feelings and observations were.

Then shift the debrief discussion from the particular experience with the group juggling game to the larger world. How have the experiences in this exercise been reflected in other experiences people have had? In what ways were these experiences similar? In what ways are these experiences different? How might the actions taken to meet the group juggling challenge provide insight for dealing with losses in other contexts?

APPENDIX C

Sermon

THIS IS A SERMON the authors have preached in many places and in different variations as a dialog sermon. This particular sermon was preached in Nagaland in northeast India under the title "Mother Courage," echoing the story of the Naga Mothers Association in chapter 10.

Text: 2 Sam 21:1–14

DAN: It's a joy to be here with you this morning. We bring you greetings from your sisters and brothers in Christ in the United States.

SHARON: This morning we want to call your attention to a strange and awful story from 2 Samuel. This is one of those awful Old Testament stories that we might read as we are working our way through the Bible just to say we've read the whole thing. We rush past it, never to revisit it again. We might even think—what an awful story! Why did God have to put *that* in the Bible? Let's get on to the really good stuff! Ah, but this story is worth another visit.

DAN: It begins with a famine plaguing Israel, and King David prays to ask God what the problem is. God says there is bloodguilt on the land. Innocent blood had been shed. Gross injustice, terrible violence, had taken place and never been addressed.

SHARON: Here's what happened. When Saul was king he massacred Gibeonites, killing in a way we would today call genocide.

The Gibeonites were an ethnic minority who had made a covenant of peace with Israel during the invasion of the Promised Land under Joshua. The story of that peace covenant is told in the book of Joshua, chapter 9. But Saul violated that covenant. Gibeonites were massacred, and God became the only advocate for these forgotten victims. After the death of Saul, David became king, coming from a different tribe within Israel. God cursed the land in which this brutality had been committed, even though it was the homeland of God's special covenant people.

DAN: So once David heard from God that Israel's guilt for this broken treaty and massacre was a problem, he met with the surviving Gibeonites to see what they could do to set things right. David and the Gibeonites chose a solution that was common back then and has continued to this day. They decided to deal with the old violence of the past by committing new violence in the present. The Gibeonites who had been so awfully wronged wanted revenge. "Give us the male descendants of Saul—kill them for us!" So David did. Seven of Saul's sons and grandsons were butchered in public, run through with huge stakes, impaled, and left out in public display. The Bible says they did this "before the Lord," as a religious act.

SHARON: But God is silent—God does not lift the curse upon the land. Evidently what David and the Gibeonites did in murdering these children was not the way God wanted the bloodguilt to be lifted.

DAN: But so often the way of the world is the way of violence. We see a problem, and like David we apply real politics to solve the problem by meeting violence with violence. We fight fire with fire. We atone for one evil by committing another. How many times, even here among the Nagas, have we seen some justify their use of violence by referring to the violence done by the other side? That group, those terrible people did that terrible thing, so we are going to kill them to set things right. You know, my mother taught me two wrongs do not make a right.

SHARON: Do Naga mothers say that? Maybe David wasn't listening to his mother when she said that. How many innocent victims do we create in our efforts to balance the books of terror? How many have been impaled in our quest for justice?

DAN: These seven descendants of Saul were innocents. They were too young to have participated in the atrocities of their father or grandfather. But like the innocent Lamb of God, like Jesus the Christ, they were impaled and hung up in public in the name of restoring the peace.

SHARON: But then, in the wake of this awful violence, a mother, a courageous mother, changes the story.

DAN: One mother, Merab, lost five sons that day. She simply disappears from the story. Merab becomes that eternal grieving, silent mother who fades away in the overwhelming sorrow of her loss. Ah, there are so many mothers, fathers, sisters, brothers, daughters, and sons like Merab. They are victims who are frozen forever in their grief and anguish. They can never move beyond the terrible loss they have suffered.

SHARON: But the other mother, Rizpah, transforms the entire story. Two of her sons were executed. She feels the sorrow just like Merab. Perhaps besides sorrow she felt anger at the injustice of her loss. But unlike Merab, Rizpah does not fade away. Rizpah instead comes out into the public space where the bodies of her sons are displayed. Rizpah with mother grief, with mother anger, with mother courage, begins a public vigil over the bodies of her boys. She spreads a rough cloth on the ground and stays there. She keeps the dogs away. She scares off the birds that circle round about. She keeps that vigil out in public, day after day, night after night.

DAN: There is only one verse about her action. That verse says she began at the start of the barley harvest and continued until the rains fell. One commentary I read said the barley harvest began in April, and the rainy season started in the fall. One verse, but many months.

SHARON: Imagine Rizpah there by the bodies of her sons—April, May, June. What is happening to those bodies?

DAN: What do the women in the town do? Maybe they say, "Rizpah, come home. You've grieved enough. It's time to get on with your life. You can't bring your children back to life by this wasting of yourself."

SHARON: But Rizpah continues—June, July, August. The bodies have disintegrated in the open air and are nearly bones now. The town's people all think she is crazy, she's a madwoman. But she continues—August, September, October.

DAN: And finally David hears about her vigil. King David hears and is moved in his heart by this mother. David comes. He comes publicly to the mother whose sons he ordered executed. He publicly gathers their bones. On his way to meet Rizpah, David also gathers the bones of Saul and his other sons who had perished in the battle of Mt. Gilboa but never been properly buried. Together, David and Rizpah bury them all appropriately and with due respect in the land of their family.

SHARON: Then God heals the land. God did not heal the land in response to David's executions. God healed the land when David reversed his policy of violence and came publicly to Rizpah. He came, I believe, in repentance and humility. David came to the sorrowing mother in her vigil, and he tenderly dealt with the bones of her children. The violence was over. The cycle of revenge and retribution was broken. Grief was given an expression that could bring healing at long last.

DAN: It's a strange story, and Rizpah's action gets just one verse. But her action transforms the whole story. David changes, and from his change, inspired by Rizpah, the land is healed. There have been many Daughters of Rizpah over the years, mothers who have turned their grief into courageous public witness to end violence and heal their lands.

SHARON: I think today of the Naga Mothers. During the head hunting days it was Naga women who sometimes mediated between the warring villages to stop the killing. The warriors are remembered and honored, but what about those women who had the courage to risk getting between the warriors to stop the violence?

DAN: I have been working with Naga peace efforts since 1996, and in that process, I quickly discovered the key role played by the Naga Mothers. The Naga Mothers Association began out of the grief over the lost lives of so many Naga young people. They would get a new shawl to wrap up the body of each Naga they retrieved from the army bases. Their grief and anger finally boiled over, and the Naga Mothers became one of the leading groups working for an end to this long-standing conflict. Too many of their children were dying.

SHARON: They began traveling to jungle headquarters of Naga factions to call them to peace. They journeyed to Delhi with other Naga community leaders on the Journey of Conscience, a nonviolent campaign calling for a negotiated settlement to the war. These Naga Mothers are Daughters of Rizpah.

DAN: I am reminded of the Mothers of the Plaza de Mayo in Argentina. During the so-called Dirty War in Argentina in the 1970s some thirty thousand people "disappeared" under the military dictatorship. The whole country was paralyzed by fear. But finally Rizpahs began to stir, grieving mothers. I can see the mothers meeting around their kitchen tables:

SHARON: "Where is Roberto? I haven't seen him for a while." "He went to university a few weeks ago and never came back. His friends have no idea where he is. Where is your Maria?" "She was taken off a bus by the police, but when I went to the station to get her, the police said they had no record of her being arrested. That was months ago."

DAN: These grieving mothers found each other, and they began to vigil. Every Thursday they would go to the Plaza de Mayo in Buenos Aires and march with photos of their children.

SHARON: Their signs read: "Where is my son? Where is my daughter?" Some people called them in Spanish *las locas*—"the crazy ones"—an epithet that I'm sure Rizpah heard in her own native Hebrew. Some of the mothers disappeared, but more took their places.

DAN: Finally those mothers became the conscience of the country and sparked a nonviolent campaign that helped bring down the dictatorship, restore democracy, and end the Dirty War. Mothers of the Disappeared in Chile under the Pinochet dictatorship made their grief public as well. Sometimes they would go to public dances and take to the dance floor alone. Their missing sons, their missing husbands, their missing fathers were the stark invisible presence with them calling out to a nation that buried its conscience under terror.

SHARON: We have a Rizpah in the United States. Her name is Cindy Sheehan. Her son Casey was killed in action in Iraq in 2004. She became a voice of protest against the war. She kept vigil as a grieving mother outside the gate of the ranch of President Bush. As a mother who lost her son in this war she has paid a price that few others in my country have paid. She has channeled her own huge loss into energy to spare other mothers the same loss she has experienced. We could go on and on. There are so many grieving mothers who have turned their sorrow into powerful voices and actions for peace. They are acting for a better world for the children still alive and those yet to be born. Do you know of any Rizpahs?

DAN: For us as Christians, however, the key question to ask is: Where was God in this Bible story? We saw God at the beginning, raising a problem to David. God brought to David's attention a terrible injustice that had not been put right. God was an advocate for those who had been victimized. But God doesn't heal the land when David and the Gibeonites take revenge. God doesn't condone matching Saul's violence with their own violence.

SHARON: Rather God comes in months later after the grieving mother Rizpah bore tragic and persistent witness to the cost of this cycle of violence. God comes in after Rizpah's vigil brings about a complete turnaround in David's kingly action. God comes in to heal the land when the cycle of violence is halted, thanks to a mother who made her grief the stopping place.

DAN: For us as Christians we recognize that God has made a stopping place for all violence, for all sin. That stopping place is the foot of the cross of Jesus Christ. When Jesus died he took upon himself the sin of the whole world, including every act of violence. He carried that sin, carried that injury, carried that wounding. Whoever truly comes to Jesus and bows at the foot of the cross has to stop the cycle of violence within them. For how can I kill someone for whom Christ has died? At the foot of the cross the violence stops.

SHARON: And just as the seven sons of Rizpah were impaled for the sins of others, Jesus was pierced for our sins. He became the one who bears all the wounds of those sinned against. He has carried in his own body the unjust suffering of all of us who have been harmed by the unjust and evil actions of others. So we who are wounded, we can let his love and grace wash over us. We can let his mercy lead us to the place of forgiveness. We can let his broken body and shed blood guide us to the place of reconciliation.

DAN: Where is God today? Is God fighting on any of the sides in this world's many conflicts that claim divine support and guidance? Is God with those who say "Nagaland for Christ," who then kill or threaten to kill because of whatever evil the other side has done?

SHARON: Or is God waiting for someone with the courage to halt the seemingly endless spirals of bloodshed? Is God waiting for someone to stand at the foot of the cross and proclaim that any killing in the name of the crucified Christ is an insult to Jesus? Is God waiting for a courageous mother or father, a sister or brother, a daughter or son to say, "Enough! My loss is beyond consolation, but I will not have vengeance taken in my name." We have to find a way to peace or we will be hopelessly lost in a maze of killing, and more killing, and yet more killing.

DAN: Rizpah calls to us amid the carnage of our warring world. Her children are gone.

SHARON: But she asks us, What will we do to ensure that our children and our grandchildren face a different future? God is waiting for our action to bring healing to the land.

DAN: My sisters and my brothers, what will you do today? Will you turn away from desires for revenge? Will you repent of the feelings of hatred, even toward those who have treated you unjustly?

SHARON: My sisters and my brothers, will you come to the foot of the cross? Will you come to say, "For me the ways of violence are not my way. My way is the way of Jesus." We can weep the tears of sorrow. We can weep the tears of anger. But we will also place our tears in the hands and heart of Jesus. We will let him change us so he can use us to bring healing to the land.

DAN: Will you commit yourself to be a Rizpah? Will you commit yourself to be a voice to call for an end to violence? Will you commit yourself to be a witness for the healing of the land, for the healing of your people?

SHARON: Let us pray that God's healing will come and bless this land. May God flow with healing among us now. May God's healing flow through us and from us into all the hills and valleys and plains around us. Come and pray.

APPENDIX D

Poetry, Art, and Rizpah

RIZPAH IS UNKNOWN IN most Western church circles, but occasionally poets and artists have articulated her heroic vigil.

Poetry

The great English poet Alfred, Lord Tennyson, wrote a poem titled "Mother of Sorrows: Rizpah,"[1] not one that is usually featured in high school or collegiate literature courses. Tennyson weaves together the biblical story referred to in the title with a more contemporary setting. He presents the grieving mother in a state of madness that brings cuttingly perceptive wisdom to the problems of the condition of the legal system in the Victorian Era. Besides the biblical story, Tennyson's poem is based on the 1793 hanging of a thief whose mother poured out her maternal love in Rizpah-like passion.

The executed son is Willy. Willy's mother screams out her grief in searing language. Like Rizpah, she drives away "the hell-black raven and horrible fowls of the air." For Willy's mother God will pardon these birds but not the lawyers who killed her son. She takes those who killed her son to task with the Bible:

> Sin? O yes—we are sinners, I know—let all that be,
> And read me a Bible verse of the Lord's good will toward men—

---

1. "Mother of Sorrows: Rizpah" is in the public domain. It can be found in Stedman, *Victorian Anthology*.

'Full of compassion and mercy, the Lord'—let me hear it again;
'Full of compassion and mercy—long-suffering.' Yes, O yes!
For the lawyer is born but to murder—the Saviour lives but to
bless.

Tennyson doesn't jump into biblical interpretation, but he clearly
sides with the mother whose child was taken unjustly.

Huub Oosterhuis is a Dutch priest, poet, and theologian.
Born in 1933, he is prolific, composing more than seven hundred
hymns, songs, and psalms as well as writing over sixty books. He
left the Roman Catholic Church but continued his writing of biblical songs and prayers, combined with his political activism. The
hymns by Oosterhuis are sung in both Catholic and Protestant
churches, though some of his works have been censored from
church settings.

One of his hymns is in the voice of Rizpah confronting the
king with his evil and expressing her trust in the ultimate justice
of God. Here is his "Song of Rizpah" ("Het Lied Van Rispa" in
Dutch)—a song unlike any we have heard in a church![2]

Song of Rizpah

Your law is evil, o king.
I will go into the mountains
I will defeat the vultures of heaven,
the jackals of the earth.
I will save my dead from their teeth,
their bodies from your hands, o king,
I will defy you.

Your law is murder, o king,
your god must be a god of death.
But there exists one on earth
with whom the dead are sheltered.
I will bear the summer heat,
the storm and the rain, o king,
I will be with them.

2. Oosterhuis, *Verzameld Liedboek*, 347. English translation by Matthijs
Kronemeijer. Used with permission.

Your law is finished, o king.
I know of new times coming,
of men and women fully living,
freed from the fate of guilt and revenge.
the trees are heavily laden with fruit,
on every mountain, high sheaves,
(a harvest) of justice.

Paintings

Though there are some paintings about Rizpah by major artists, none of them are among their best known works. Some lesser known illustrators have also captured the story of Rizpah, though that story is seldom depicted in collections of biblical stories.

George Becker is a lesser-known American artist; there isn't even a Wikipedia article about him. However, Becker painted *Rizpah Protecting the Bodies of Her Sons*[3] in 1875 (see next page). The painting was first shown at the 1876 US Centennial Exhibition in Philadelphia. Becker depicts Rizpah with heroic energy fighting off a huge scavenger bird with Saul's slain descendants hanging high behind her. She wields a long stick, drawn back to slash at the bird as with a sword. Rizpah's cape and dress ripple in the wind behind her. For all its gruesomeness this is our favorite painting about Rizpah because it shows her passion and strength with intense dynamism.

Frederic Lord Leighton (1830–96) was the first British painter to be granted a peerage. He died the next day, making his the shortest-lived peerage. Many of Leighton's paintings cover biblical themes. His *Rizpah* depicts the grieving mother in a black dress with a sickle in one hand while with the other she reaches protectively around the bound body of one of her sons. Three of the bodies are depicted, with their arms draped over the cross beams on which they had been raised and executed. The heads of the dead hang down and are covered by long cloths, perhaps placed there by

---

3. George Becker's *Rizpah Protecting the Bodies of Her Sons* is in the public domain.

Rizpah to protect their faces from the birds. Dark vultures loom above like evil slashes in the sky. Two leopards lurk menacingly behind a tree in the background.

J. M. W. Turner (1775–1851), another British artist, was known for his romantic watercolors, shimmering atmosphere, and frequent dark landscapes and seascapes. Turner's *Rispah*[4] captures the bleakness of the story with black and dark reddish hues. A skeletal crescent moon looks down from the evening sky. The bodies of Rizpah's and Merab's sons lie rotting on the ground with Rizpah sitting in the center. Her grief isn't as frenetic and powerful as in the depictions by other artists, but Turner seems to capture the long, exhausting, yet persistent nature of Rizpah's vigil.

James Tissot (1836–1902) was a French painter and illustrator. He worked alongside other Impressionist artists such as Degas and Manet. In 1885 Tissot experienced a renewal of his Catholic faith that led him to depict more scenes from the Bible in his art. His last major project was a huge series of paintings about Old Testament themes, including *The Kindness of Rizpah*. The five bodies of the sons of Saul hang on a line of crosses while Rizpah stands in front fending off giant birds. Rizpah is portrayed as fairly young, perhaps in her 30s or 40s. She stands with feet spread brandishing a long palm frond to swat at the large black vultures diving down upon her. Spread on the ground is a brown and white cloth with other cloths, perhaps garments or rugs, in a pile nearby. Snow-capped mountains tower in the background.

Fabric Art

Rev. Cindy Weber of the Jeff Street Baptist Community at Liberty in Louisville, Kentucky, introduced us to Rizpah at a Bible study she led at a summer conference for the Baptist Peace Fellowship of North America in Oberlin, Ohio, in 2001. Rizpah continued to inspire her, so Rev. Weber quilted a powerful piece of fabric art about Rizpah titled *Keeping the Beasts at Bay*.[5]

Blue is the dominant color of her depiction. Rizpah stands in outline in the lower center of the quilt with hands upraised. Black

4. *Rispah*—with the British spelling of the name—is the property of the Tate Britain Museum in London but is seldom put on display.

5. Shown with permission of Cindy Weber.

birds cloud the sky at the top. An arc of bright multicolored swirls seem to be coming from Rizpah making a protective shield of her love and passion. Weber's artistic expression is full of energy, affirming life while surrounded by death.

BIBLIOGRAPHY

This bibliography is not meant to be an exhaustive list of books about trauma, trauma recovery, and trauma transformation. Rather we wish to share with readers the books we have found most helpful both academically and personally, including those used or referred to in *Daughters of Rizpah*.

'Ali, 'Abdullah Yusuf, ed. *The Meaning of the Holy Qur'an*. Beltsville, MD: amana, 2001.

Allender, Dan B. *The Wounded Heart: Hope for Adult Victims of Childhood Sexual Abuse and the Hope of Transformation*. Colorado Springs: NavPress, 1994.

Arnold, Bill T. *1 & 2 Samuel*. NIV Application Commentary. Grand Rapids: Zondervan, 2003.

Baldwin, Joyce G. *1 & 2 Samuel: An Introduction & Commentary*. Tyndale Old Testament Commentaries. Downers Grove, IL: InterVarsity, 1988.

Barker, Paul A., ed. *Tackling Trauma: Global, Biblical, and Pastoral Perspectives*. Carlisle, UK: Langham Partnership, 2019.

Bass, Ellen, and Laura Davis. *The Courage to Heal: A Guide for Women Survivors of Child Sexual Abuse*. New York: Harper & Row, 1988.

Bergen, Robert D. *1, 2 Samuel*. New American Commentary: An Exegetical and Theological Exposition of Holy Scripture. Nashville: Broadman & Holman, 1996.

Blades, Lincoln Anthony. "Trauma From Slavery Can Actually Be Passed Down Through Your Genes." *Teen Vogue*, May 31, 2016. https://www.teenvogue.com/story/slavery-trauma-inherited-genetics.

Buttry, Dan. *Blessed Are the Peacemakers*. Canton, MI: Read the Spirit, 2011.

———. *Peace Warrior: A Memoir from the Front*. Macon, GA: Mercer University Press, 2012.

———. *We Are the Socks*. Canton, MI: Read the Spirit, 2015.

Cherry, Stephen. *Healing Agony: Re-imagining Forgiveness*. London: Continuum, 2012.

Frazer, Jenni. "Wiesel: Yes We Really Did Put God on Trial." *The Jewish Chronicle*, September 19, 2008.

Glaser, Ida. "A Trauma Observed: Biblical Reflections on Safety, Control and Fragmentation." In *Tackling Trauma: Global, Biblical, and Pastoral Perspectives*, edited by Paul A. Barker, 51–82. Carlisle, UK: Langham Partnership, 2019.

Goldman, Francisco. "Children of the Dirty War: Argentina's Stolen Orphans." *The New Yorker*, March 12, 2012. https://www.newyorker.com/magazine/2012/03/19/children-of-the-dirty-war.

Keen, Sam. *Faces of the Enemy: Reflections of the Hostile Imagination*. New York: Harper & Row, 1986.

Keil, C. F., and F. Delitzsch. *Biblical Commentary on the Books of Samuel*. Grand Rapids: Eerdmans, 1950.

Krist, Jan. "Hope." New York: American Society of Composers, Authors and Publishers, 2008.

Levine, Peter A. *Healing Trauma: A Pioneering Program for Restoring the Wisdom of Your Body*. Boulder, CO: Sounds True, 2005.

———. *In an Unspoken Voice: How the Body Releases Trauma and Restores Goodness*. Berkeley, CA: North Atlantic, 2010.

———. *Waking the Tiger, Healing Trauma: The Innate Capacity to Transform Overwhelming Experiences*. Berkeley, CA: North Atlantic, 1997.

McAllister, Pam. *You Can't Kill the Spirit*. Philadelphia: New Society, 1988.

Mellibovsky, Matilde. *Circle of Love Over Death: Testimonies of the Mothers of the Plaza de Mayo*. Williamantic, CT: Curbstone, 1997.

Mohn, Bent. "Talk with Isak Dinesen." *New York Times*, November 3, 1957.

Oosterhuis, Huub. *Verzameld Liedboek*. Kampen, Netherlands: Kok, 2004.

Pray the Devil Back to Hell. Produced by Abigail E. Disney. Directed by Gini Reticker. Fork Films, 2008. DVD, 72 minutes.

Remembering Srebrenica. "Remembering Srebrenica mourns the death of Mother of Srebrenica, Hatidža Mehmedović." https://www.srebrenica.org.uk/news/death-of-hatidza-mehmedovic/.

Rendon, Jim. *Upside: The New Science of Post-Traumatic Growth*. New York: Touchstone, 2015.

Roberts, Stephen B., and Willard W. C. Ashley Sr., eds. *Disaster Spiritual Care: Practical Clergy Responses to Community, Regional, and National Tragedy*. Woodstock, VT: Skylight Paths, 2015.

Saikia, Arunbh. "The Mothers of Nagaland Are Taking It Upon Themselves to Keep the Peace—Yet Again." *Scroll.in*, November 25, 2019. https://scroll.in/article/943445/the-mothers-of-nagaland-are-taking-it-upon-themselves-to-keep-the-peace-yet-again.

Sheehan, Cindy. *Dear President Bush*. San Francisco: City Lights, 2006.

———. *Not One More Mother's Child*. Kihei, Maui, HI: Koa, 2005.

———. *Peace Mom*. New York: Atria, 2006.

Silverman, Steven M. "President Bush Will Not Meet Grieving Mom." *People*, August 12, 2005.

Sinha, Dipanjan. "The Crusader on a New Battle." *The Telegraph, On-Line Edition*, February 20, 2013. https://www.telegraphindia.com/states/northeast/the-crusader-on-a-new-battle/cid/336049.

Surk, Barbara. "Hatidža Mehmedović, 65, Dies: Spoke Out for Bosnia Massacre Victims." *New York Times*, July 27, 2018.

Tennyson, Alfred Lord. "Mother of Sorrows: Rizpah." In *A Victorian Anthology, 1837–1895*, edited by Edmund Clarence Stedman, 209–11. Cambridge: Riverside, 1895.

Thompson, R. J. *Penitence and Sacrifice in Early Israel Outside the Levitical Law*. Leiden: Brill, 1963.

"To End Bloodshed, Naga Mothers Walk the Long Road to Peace." *The Naga Republic*, August 19, 2018. https://www.thenagarepublic.com/features/to-end-bloodshed-naga-mothers-walk-the-long-road-to-peace/.

Trible, Phyllis. *Texts of Terror: Literary-Feminist Readings of Biblical Narratives*. Philadelphia: Fortress, 1984.

Tula, Maria Teresa. *Hear My Testimony*. Edited and translated by Lynn Stephen. Boston: South End, 1994.

Tushima, Cephas T. A. *The Fate of Saul's Progeny in the Reign of David*. Cambridge: James Clark, 2011.

Van der Kolk, Bessel A. *The Body Keeps the Score: Brain, Mind, and Body in the Healing of Trauma*. New York: Viking, 2014.

Walsh, David. "'This Anti-Russia Campaign Is Horrible': An Interview with Antiwar Activist Cindy Sheehan." World Socialist Website, October 23, 2017. https://www.wsws.org/en/articles/2017/10/23/shee-023.html.

Wiesel, Elie. *The Trial of God*. New York: Schocken, 1979.

Wikipedia. "Naga Mothers Association." Last modified September 3, 2019. https://en.wikipedia.org/wiki/Naga_Mothers_Association.

Yehuda, Rachel. "How Trauma and Resilience Cross Generations." *On Being with Krista Tippett*, July 30, 2015. https://onbeing.org/programs/rachel-yehuda-how-trauma-and-resilience-cross-generations-nov2017/.

Youngblood, Ronald F. *1 & 2 Samuel*. Expositor's Bible Commentary. Grand Rapids: Zondervan, 2010.